Messages In Your Tea Cup

Learn to read tea leaves

Messages In Your Tea Cup

Learn to read tea leaves

Irene McGarvie

Ancient Wisdom Publishing
a division of Nixon-Carre Ltd., Toronto, ON

Copyright © 2009 by Irene McGarvie

All rights reserved. No part of this book may be reproduced or transmitted in any form or by any means, electronic or mechanical, including photocopying and recording, or by any information storage or retrieval system without written permission from the author, except for brief passages quoted in a review.

Library and Archives Canada Cataloguing in Publication

McGarvie, Irene, 1957-
    Messages in your tea cup : learn to read tea leaves / Irene McGarvie.

Includes index.
ISBN 978-0-9783939-6-0

    1. Fortune-telling by tea leaves. I. Title.
BF1881.M34 2009   133.3'244
C2009-901581-1

Published by:
Ancient Wisdom Publishing
A division of Nixon-Carre Ltd.
P.O. Box 92533
Carlton RPO
Toronto, Ontario, M5A 4N9

www.learnancientwisdom.com
www.nixon-carre.com

Distributed by Ingram 1-800-937-8000
www.ingrambook.com

Disclaimer:
This publication is designed to provide accurate and authoritative information. It is sold with the understanding that the publishers are not engaged in rendering legal, medical or other professional advice. If medical or other expert assistance is required, the services of a competent professional should be sought. The information contained herein represents the experiences and opinions of the author, but the author is not responsible for the results of any action taken on the basis of information in this work, nor for any errors or omissions.

General Notice:
Any product names used in this book are for identification purposes only and may be registered trademarks, or trade names of their respective owners. The author, Irene McGarvie, and the publisher, Ancient Wisdom Publishing (a division of Nixon-Carre Ltd.) disclaim any and all rights in those marks.

Cover image www.istockphoto.com   **Printed and bound in the USA**

"There is no trouble so great or grave that cannot be much diminished by a nice cup of tea."

Bernard-Paul Heroux

This book is dedicated to my mother

Jane McGarvie

Not a day goes by that I don't wish I could sit and have a cup of tea with you.

With special thanks to all the people who helped with suggestions, encouragement and proofreading:

Jacqlyn Avis
Mike Morley
Chantal Patenaude
Sue Rogge
Sharon Russell

Contents

Chapter 1 - Tasseography 1

Pictures in a cup • Reading coffee grounds • Use your imagination • What is intuition? Where are these messages coming from? • What is the difference between a psychic and a medium? • Our minds always try to make sense out of abstract images • Reading tea leaves helps you to understand yourself better • How does it work when reading for others? • Does it really work? • What is so special about tea? • Tea leaf reading offers other benefits to the reader

Chapter 2 - Everyone Can Read Tea Leaves 13

Dispelling the myths • This isn't a special gift • Every child is psychic • This isn't a curse, it is a blessing • The importance of ritual • Psychometry • Do you have to start with a prayer? • Is it dangerous? • Never look into another person's future without their consent • How often can you consult the tea leaves? • Crisis and calamity in your tea cup • Censoring your comments • Everyone wants to know the same things

Chapter 3 - All About Tea 27

The history of tea • Myths about tea • Tea in Japan • Tea arrives in the west • Tea incites rebellion • A guide to the different types of tea • What exactly is tea? • Harvesting and processing tea • Black tea • Post-fermented tea • Green tea • Oolong tea • White tea • Kukicha • Rooiboos • Blended teas • Flavoured teas • Herbal Infusions and tisanes

Chapter 4 - Tea Leaf Reading in 10 Steps **39**

Chapter 5 - Tea Leaf Reading as a Business **47**

Is it legal where you live? • Insurance coverage • Disturbing developments in Britain • 20th century witch hunt • Lawsuits and other legal headaches • Asking clients to sign a release • Audio recordings of your sessions • Privacy laws and your client files • Limit how often you will read for a client • Charging for your services • Dealing with skeptics • Building your business • There is no competition • Home parties • Coffee shops, restaurants, book stores, and bars • Psychic fairs • Outdoor fairs and street festivals • Keep everything legal

Chapter 6 - Meditation **67**

Focusing your mind throught meditation • Music or silence? • Meditation posture • Mindfulness meditation • Concentration meditation • Monkey mind • Breath meditation • Candle flame • Meditating on a rose • Morphing shapes • Number concentration • Dealing with distractions • How long should I meditate? • The sit-stand method

Chapter 7 - Symbolism **77**

Chapter 8 - Sample Readings **117**

Appendix A - Money Symbols **135**
Appendix B - Love Symbols **137**
Appendix C - Children Symbols **139**
Appendix D - Health Symbols **140**
Appendix E - Honesty Symbols **141**

Index **144**

1

Tasseography

Pictures in a cup

The word Tasseography comes from the French word tasse (cup) and the Greek word graph (which refers to drawing or pictures). So Tasseography simply means pictures in a cup.

Tea leaf reading, or Tasseography, is a method of divination that involves interpreting the meanings of images and symbols that appear in the tea leaves remaining in a cup after the tea has been consumed. Similar divination methods include looking at the images produced by flames in a fire, by throwing pebbles on sand, or by dropping hot wax into cold water. In many ancient cultures it was customary to look for signs and symbols predicting future events by examining the entrails of slaughtered animals.

Ancient Romans practiced a similar form of divination which involved interpreting the sediment left on the bottom of an empty wine cup. But before you decide that reading wine sounds like more fun than reading tea leaves keep in mind that this method of divination only worked back in the days when there actually was sediment left in the bottom of the glass. Our modern methods of filtering wine mean that there is nothing left in the bottom of the glass to read.

Reading coffee grounds

In cultures where coffee is the primary beverage of choice, such as the Mediterranean, the Middle East, and Latin America, people developed methods of reading the coffee grounds. To read coffee grounds you simply brew coffee using ground coffee beans without a filter, and when you pour the cup of coffee you allow some of the grounds to pour into the cup.

Tea leaves and coffee grounds are simply tools. There is no magic in the tools themselves. Regardless of which tool you use, the method is pretty much the same. The reader sees an image and then interprets what that symbol means.

It is not quite as easy as it sounds, it takes some practice because first the reader must recognize the images, then interpret the meaning of each of the images and then combine the meanings into a logical message. This requires imagination and intuition. Imagination allows the reader to see the images, and then intuition guides you to the correct interpretation.

Use your imagination

The imagination part is the difficult part for most people. The first time you look into a tea cup your initial thought is that all you see is a blob of tea leaves. The key is to relax, have a little fun, and let the images flow.

Do you remember lying on the grass looking up at

the clouds as a child? Small children have such wonderful imaginations that they immediately begin to see pictures in the clouds. However, we soon learn to suppress our imaginations in order to fit in at school and in society. The key to tea leaf reading is to release the imaginative child inside of you.

What do you see?

In the above picture there are 8 different images. Do you see them? Don't read any further until you have found at least 2 different images. You know the images are in there, it is just a matter of relaxing and they will jump out at you.

Don't worry, this isn't a test. There is no correct answer.

A hundred different people can look at this abstract image and see a hundred different images.

Actually, this exercise was just a trick. There is nothing special about this picture, I did not insert any special images. I created a random bunch of cloud like shapes in a few minutes with the airbrush tool in photoshop. The point was to show you that if you tell yourself that the images are there, if you expect to see something, you will begin to see them.

What is intuition? Where are these ideas coming from?

We all have intuition. The only difference between someone who considers themselves to be "psychic" and someone who doesn't, is that the psychic has learned to listen to and trust their intuition.

Exactly what intuition is, and where the information comes from is difficult to prove conclusively. I think that it is likely that sometimes we are accessing information that is stored somewhere in the dark recesses of our mind, the result of our own past experiences or things we have read, but something we do not consciously remember.

Sometimes we are "simply" reading the body language and the energy around the person that we are reading for. This is the explanation that most skeptics prefer, suggesting that this is some sort of "cheating". I have accentuated the word "simply" because it is not quite as "simple" as most skeptics would have you believe. Regardless, if the reader is sincere and is in no way attempting to manipulate or defraud anyone, and if the message received in this way benefits the person you are reading for, then I don't think it really matters where the information came from.

But often the information definitely comes from outside of us. Things we could not possibly know. Where does it come from? There seems to be a universal consciousness, superconscious mind, or universal mind that each of us can access. I think that this is where most inventions or other great ideas come from, which explains why two people who have had no contact with one another, who live on opposite sides of the world will come up with the same invention at the same time.

Everyone has at one time or another had a really good idea for an invention, a book, or a business, something that you were sure would be a real winner. But you never did anything about it and sure enough some time later you hear that someone else is making a fortune with "your" idea. How did that happen? Did they steal your idea? No, probably not, it seems that there are ideas floating by us all the time in some sort of cloud or stream. Sometimes we grab those ideas, pluck them out of the ether and use them. Other times we ignore them and they just float right by. Developing your intuition means learning to intentionally gain access to this superconscious or universal mind.

Spirit Guides

Sometimes the source of this information seems to have an individual identity, as though a particular person is giving you the answers. Often, people who experience getting information this way refer to the source of the information as their "Spirit Guide". It is like having a conversation in your head with another person.

So what is the difference between having a Spirit Guide

and suffering from schizophrenia? Well basically, the primary difference is that with Spirit Guides you are in control. They might give you helpful suggestions, but they do not tell you what to do. It is a pleasant supportive arrangement, not one where strange voices are telling you to hurt yourself or someone else.

It is not even necessary to actually believe that you are talking to a separate individual, you can assume that you are just making it up, and it will still work. Depending on your religious or cultural background you can also choose to believe that a particular religious or historic figure is the one giving you the information.

It makes me really uncomfortable when I hear people say things like "Spirit told me to tell you...." or "Spirit says I have to...." as if they have no choice. We are always in control. We may welcome some advice, but what we choose to do with the information is up to us to decide.

What is the difference between a psychic and a medium?

The topic of this book is tea leaf reading, which is a method of using your intuition or your psychic abilities, while mediumship involves making contact with the spirits of people who have passed away (talking to dead people). John Edwards and James Van Praagh are examples of famous mediums, while people who read tarot cards and tea leaves are considered psychics.

There is a lot of confusion about the distinction between these two skills. The difference is in where the information is coming from. Psychics generally get their information from the universal mind/universal consciousness, while mediums talk directly with the spirit of a person who has passed over.

Developing your psychic abilities is an excellent first step in developing mediumship, learning to reach across and contact people on the other side. But that is definitely the topic for another book.

The religion of Spiritualism

As a Spiritualist, I believe that there is no death, that what we think of as death is simply a change of energy, discarding a worn out physical body and releasing the spirit inside. I believe that our loved ones are busy with their own new lives but they still care about us and check in with us from time to time. Connecting with people on the other side has been described as being like a two way radio with a lot of static, or trying to see someone on the other side of a really thick curtain, or hear someone under water. Sometimes it is clearer than others.

Although mediumship is not the topic of this book, the reason I am mentioning this here is because the topics of Spiritualism and mediumship manage to creep in to all of my writing and so it is inevitable that there will be references to it throughout this book and I want to make sure that you understand the distinction.

It is not necessary to be a Spiritualist in order to successfully read tea leaves. In fact, reading tea leaves has absolutely nothing to do with Spiritualism and is almost frowned on, or at least considered unnecessary among many Spiritualists.

Our minds always try to make sense out of abstract images

Recognizing images and tuning in to the superconscious or universal mind is a natural thing for people to do, we are all hard-wired to do this, although most of us do not even realize that we are doing it.

When you look into a tea cup your mind is working to recognize images or patterns in something that is abstract. Not just when we read tea leaves, we do it continually every day, it is an important life skill. This is how we make sense of the people, things and events around us. People who have had particular parts of their brains damaged and loose this ability are at a definite disadvantage in life.

Recognizing images is a highly personal and subjective process. Two people looking at the same blob of tea leaves often see entirely different things. One person might see a squirrel while another person sees a rooster, one person might see a shell while another person sees a bush.

Try this test with a friend. Look up at some clouds and then each of you secretly write down the list of images you saw, then look at each other's list. You will be amazed at the differences between your two lists.

How is it that two people looking at the same clouds can see such different things? It is because we tend to see only the things that make sense to us based on our own life experiences.

Reading tea leaves helps you to understand yourself better

When reading for ourselves we tend to recognize symbols that relate to the issue that we are most concerned with at the moment. Have you ever seen or taken a Rorschach test? This is where you look at an ink blot and say what pops into your mind. This is similar to what happens when you read tea leaves. This abstract pattern recognition accesses our subconscious mind and helps us to understand what we are not even aware that we are thinking of. Therefore, reading for yourself helps you to understand yourself better.

How does it work when reading for others?

When reading for other people you must be able to tune in to the concerns of the person you are reading for, not letting your own issues color what you are seeing. In this case you are not accessing your own mind, but the mind of the person you are reading for, along with the superconscious or universal mind, which is the repository of all knowledge past, present, and future. How adept we become at accessing this universal mind determines the accuracy of our readings.

Does it really work?

Absolutely! As you practice doing it for yourself and others you will be astonished at how well it works.

Is it 100% accurate all the time? No, it is never completely accurate, which is one of the reasons why you have to be careful how you word your predictions. There is no point in upsetting someone regarding something that might not take place. Sometimes it is inaccurate because the reader was having an off day and wasn't able to tune in properly. Other times I think it is because there are some things we just aren't meant to know at the time.

What is so special about tea?

Since we know there are lots of materials that can be read to get messages, what is so special about tea? For people with a strong connection to the British Isles, tea is comfort, love, family, relaxation and much more. Getting together with loved ones always involved putting on the kettle. I've been drinking it since I could sip it from a cup.

It is this comfort, relaxation, and connection with loved ones that tea provides, combined with the fact that loose tea makes such clear pictures, that makes it so ideal for divination. That and of course the fact that in the past every home in Britain had all the necessary tools readily at hand.

Tea drinking is not intimidating like some other forms of divination. There are no frightening images like there are on some tarot decks, nor does it require a dark and mysterious environment as in mirror gazing.

Tea leaf reading offers other benefits to the reader

Besides predicting events in the future, tea leaf reading provides many other benefits to the reader. As I have already mentioned, tea leaf reading can help you to understand yourself better by enabling you to discover hidden concerns that you didn't even realize you were thinking about.

Many of us, at least occasionally, indulge in self

destructive behavior. Why is that? Self analysis through tea leaf reading can help you to recognize, understand, and possibly change your behavior.

Are you an artist? Developing your ability to read tea leaves will make you a more creative person. Regardless of the type of art you create, whether it is visual art, writing, or music, using tea leaf reading to release the imaginative child inside of you can help you in your creative endeavors.

Freeing up your intuition is useful in just about every part of life. Police use "hunches" all the time, so do auditors. What business person wouldn't want a little extra help with their business decisions? I'm sure you can think of plenty of times where intuition could come in handy for you.

"The mere chink of cups and saucers tunes the mind to happy repose."

George Gissing
The Private Papers of Henry Ryecroft

2
Anyone Can Learn to Read Tea Leaves

Let's dispel a few myths

Anyone can learn to read tea leaves. Sure, just like everything else in life, some people seem to be able to do it more easily than others, but everyone can learn to do it to some degree. The ability to tap into psychic abilities or get messages from the other side, is not just a "gift" that a few people have, we all have it. As I explained in the previous chapter, our minds are designed to enable us to tune in to messages from the super-conscious or universal mind.

This isn't a special gift that God gives to special people

I laugh when I hear that someone has a special gift, or that someone comes from a long line of psychics or mediums. When I read someone's promotional materials that indicate that they were born with this "gift" I notice that they don't mention all the time they spent practicing to perfect it.

Sure, Tiger Woods is a phenomenal golfer, he has a "gift", but he has been practicing since he could first hold a toy golf club, and he still spends most of his time practicing. He wasn't this good the first time he tried golfing. You probably won't be as good as you can be the first time you look into a tea cup either, but you will get messages, and they will be accurate enough to encourage you to keep practicing. Who knows, maybe you will turn out to be the Tiger Woods of tea leaf readers. You won't know until you try.

I know from reading the biographies of famous mediums that they all had to practice and fine tune their abilities. James Van Praagh and John Edwards are two who immediately come to mind. Now I realize that reading tea leaves isn't the same as being a medium, but it too is something that anyone can learn to do.

I cringe when I hear people say that they inherited their "gift". What if no one in your family has ever read tea leaves, does that mean that you couldn't possibly have inherited the "gift"?

Well first of all, I seriously doubt that no one in your family tree ever did this. It may not have been tea leaf reading, it might have been chicken bones, dice, rune stones, tarot cards, mirror gazing, or any of the other methods that people have used to tap into advice from the other side. People throughout history, of every race and culture, have been fascinated by the possibility of "telling the future" or "getting messages from the other side" and so it is very unlikely that no one in your family ever tried it.

Unfortunately, since it has been frowned on by the church throughout history, most of the time they kept quiet about it. It was probably something that was whispered about by the adults, definitely not something to be discussed with the kids.

Since every one of us has the "gift", I suppose in a sense we all inherited it from our ancestors.

Every child is psychic

Until about the age of five or six, every child is able to tune into the universal mind.

Look at art created by preschoolers. At this point they are the most creative that most of them will ever be in their lives. Look at the way preschoolers use colour in the pictures they create, anything is possible. They are creative and intuitive until about the time they go to school and begin to understand that there are "right" and "wrong" ways to draw pictures. By puberty most kids are so strongly influenced by peer pressure that their creativity is severely stifled.

Many children have "imaginary" friends. I know a child who from the age of about 2 ½ amazed everyone with her ability to see and speak to deceased relatives, people she had never met in life. This from a child growing up in a family where the adults are not Spiritualists and who were not even aware that is was possible to make contact with those who have passed over. As I write this, she is not quite six, so it remains to be seen whether her "gift" remains intact. I think it will depend on her degree of self-confidence (so far she has an abundance!) and whether she is able to ignore the people who try to tell her that she is making it up, that this sort of thing is not "normal" and that it is time for her to "grow out of it".

This isn't a curse, it is a blessing

I occasionally hear psychics or mediums moan and complain about what a burden their "gift" is. Well if you don't enjoy doing it, or don't feel that you are helping people, then turn it off.

We control when we consult the tea leaves, and we control what we choose to do with the information that we receive. If you find yourself getting too good at getting psychic information and you get information about people or situations that you would rather not know, or at inconvenient times, then simply turn it off; make a conscious choice not to receive the information, or only to receive it when you ask for it. This is where the importance of ritual comes in.

The importance of ritual

It is a good idea to develop a ritual that you perform whenever you decide to consult the tea leaves. The way you set out the materials, whether or not you begin with a prayer, or which way you swirl the tea residue around in the cup before you pour it out can all be part of your ritual.

There is no magic in the ritual, but by performing one you are telling your subconscious mind that it is time to go to work, that you are about to connect with the universal mind. Even the act of pulling out your special tea cups out of the cupboard, or putting out a particular table cloth serves as a sign to your subconscious mind that you are looking for some specific answers. If you believe in "Spirit Guides" your ritual serves to call them to you.

By having a particular ritual that you adhere to you are far less likely to be bothered by getting psychic information at inopportune times. It is like a store keeper putting out an open sign, your subconscious mind and your "Spirit Guides" know that you are ready to do business.

Obviously, if a particular situation was serious enough to warrant it, you would still be able to get messages when you weren't open for business, but this would be a very rare event, and only if it was in your best interest. It would be like if a storekeeper had a closed sign up, but a bystander noticed that the roof was on fire they would probably disregard the closed sign and bang on the door to warn any occupants.

A simple ritual

While it is possible to read tea leaves at the spur of the moment out of styrofoam cups, many people choose to have special tea cups and saucers that they keep just for reading. These should have white or light coloured interiors and gently sloping sides (mugs don't work as well because it is more difficult to see the images on straight sides). Keep these cups separate from your day to day dishes and use them only when you are planning to read the tea leaves.

These don't have to be new cups and saucers. Antique ones or unique ones that you bought at a flea market are great. If you are fortunate enough to inherit some from a relative that you loved this is even better because every time you use them you are likely to invoke that person's loving energy.

Psychometry

Take your time when you are buying used or antique tea cups. Take a few moments to hold each one in your hand and see how they feel. Does the cup feel good? Do any images pop into your mind? Articles often hold the energy of a particular person or event, particularly if there was strong emotion involved.

Reading the energy in an article is called Psychometry. Try it as you browse through antique stores, gently touching the articles you will find yourself more attracted to some things than others, and you might actually get a sense of the person that originally owned the article, or of a particular event that took place near the article. I think that sometimes antique tea cups actually choose their owner by attracting the person to them by their energy.

Fortunately, because the act of drinking tea is so pleasant, tea cups usually hold only warm, loving, happy energy. However, I have occasionally experienced tea cups that felt lonely or depressed. If you happen to have a tea cup whose energy doesn't feel right it is possible to improve the energy by washing and drying it carefully and letting it sit for a few days in a sunny window, surrounded by plants is ideal. Sunshine does wonders for people's moods and it works for tea cups as well.

Do you have to start with a prayer?

No, prayer is not a pre-requisite to reading tea leaves. Whether or not you would want to pray would depend on your personal religious beliefs. Effectively, what you are doing when you pray is you are setting your intention, which is to get help from the universe.

If you adhere to a particular religious tradition you might want to invoke the help and guidance of some particular entity. Wiccans often choose to invoke the help and guidance of the Mother Goddess, or earth energy. A Christian might choose to ask for Jesus' help (I know that you are probably thinking that Christians don't read tea leaves, but you would be very surprised to find out how many actually do). A Catholic might ask Mother Mary or a particular saint for help.

As a Spiritualist I usually begin with a prayer of sorts. I ask that the Infinite Spirit or Universal Energy (God) help me to understand the images I am seeing and guide me in saying the right things so that everything I say is in the best interest of the person I am reading for. In other words, it is to remind me to be careful of what I say if I am reading for others. It also serves to tell my subconscious mind and my "Spirit Guides" that we are about to start.

Whether you would say the prayer out loud or not would obviously depend on the circumstances. Are you sitting in a public place like a coffee shop? Probably best to do it silently. Are you in the privacy of your home with a person who is a little nervous that you are invoking demons? In that case you would be best to explain what you are doing and pray using the words God or Infinite Spirit to reassure them.

The closing ritual

By performing some sort of closing ritual you are telling your subconscious mind that you are finished. Your closing ritual can be something as simple as saying "That is it, that's all that I see." Then wash and dry the tea cups and put them away. This is what I do.

Some people really like to be more dramatic than that with their rituals, which is fine if that is what you prefer, but it isn't necessary. Some people like to wear flowing robes, light candles, cast protective circles of salt on the floor, etc., then ritually sweep up the salt and blow out the candles to end the ritual. There is nothing wrong with choosing to perform a more elaborate ritual, my only concern is that by doing so there is a tendency to attribute more magic and danger to what really is a natural process.

Is it dangerous?

Generally no, tea leaf reading is not dangerous. Yes, it is true that tapping into the universal consciousness does open you up to a world that none of us completely understands, and perhaps there are negative energies out there, (according to Native American teachings there are trickster spirits who will try to deceive you) but generally you tend to attract to yourself the same kind of energy you project out. Your intention is the key. Is your intention to get a little advice, and maybe a little insight into your future? There is no harm in that. The danger comes when you become too dependent on this advice and consult the tea leaves about everything.

Some people love drama and crisis. Perhaps they have

watched too many horror films depicting demonic possession and they fear that by doing anything associated with the Spirit world they are opening themselves up to something dangerous. Also, many people have religious beliefs that make them frightened, and fear is a powerful emotion that can draw negative experiences to you. so for people with these kinds of beliefs it is probably best to avoid reading tea leaves. Also, people with severe psychological or emotional problems should get help before they start dabbling in this, but for the average person who has enough self confidence, who is able to maintain a balanced life, and is not hampered by fears of the unknown, tea leaf reading is perfectly safe.

However, tea leaf reading can be dangerous if you attempt to use it to try and manipulate another person. Never use tea leaf reading as an opportunity to try to enforce your ideas upon another person. None of us really know what is best for another person. Even though you may be convinced that you know what is best for them, you cannot make choices for another person, if you attempt to it will only hurt the other person and will backfire on you.

Never look into another person's future without their consent

Doing a psychic reading for someone without their consent is a violation of their privacy. Just as you would never snoop around in someone's purse or their diary without their permission you should never consult the tea leaves for someone without their consent. Certainly, you can look for answers to questions in your own life and the situation might involve other people, but to look into a situation that doesn't involve you is a violation of the other persons' privacy. Anything that you do to someone else will eventually come back to you.

How often can you consult the tea leaves?

If you are reading for yourself you can do it as often as you like, however it is likely to be futile to consult the tea leaves more than once a day. If you do it more often than that there is unlikely to be any additional useful information and the message will tend to be jumbled and confusing.

If you are reading for someone else, a friend or a loved one, it is probably best not to do it more than once a week. If the person you are reading for is a client, it is probably best to refuse to read for them more than once a month. Everyone wants help and advice, but it is important not to allow them to become too dependent upon you. Our lives are meant to be an adventure and a learning experience, and this involves making our own decisions and living with the consequences of those decisions.

Crisis and calamity in your tea cup

What if you see something negative in a tea cup? If you are reading for yourself and you see something that looks like a terrible calamity or death there are two possibilities, either this is a reflection of something that you are worried about that may or may not take place, or it is a warning to you to make some changes to avoid a problem. You will never get a warning about something that you cannot avoid.

The important thing to remember is that nothing is written in stone. Just because you get a warning about something does not mean that it will definitely happen. All it takes is one tiny event that causes a chain reaction which could completely change the course of history.

Censoring your comments

I think that since there is always the possibility that you might be wrong there is no point in worrying someone needlessly. Even if you are right the only reason for it to be there is as a warning regarding something that can be prevented so frame your response accordingly. If you think you see a car accident perhaps you could suggest that they have their car serviced, or suggest that they change their usual pattern by taking a different route to work. Never tell someone that you see a car accident in their future. Believing that something will happen can actually cause the event to take place, and you do not want to be responsible for planting a belief like that in someone's head.

Never predict someone's death

Never predict serious illness or injury

Never diagnose health problems or prescribe treatment

Everyone wants to know the same things

I can pretty well guarantee that everyone who wants a reading wants to know the same five things. It doesn't matter who you are, these are universal human concerns:

 **Money** - Is my job secure? Am I going to find a job? Am I going to make money? Will my business be a success? Will I get a new house? Will I get a new car?

Love - Is the person I am with the right one? Is my partner faithful? Does he/she love me? Will we get married?

 **Children** - How many children will I have? When am I going to have a baby? Will I have a boy or a girl? Will my children be successful in their careers?

Health - Questions about one's own health or the health of a loved one. These are really tricky things to answer for other people, I think you would be better not to answer health questions for others, but for yourself you can certainly look for answers in your tea cup.

 **Honesty** - Is my business partner cheating me? Am I being told the truth about a particular situation? Is my lover cheating on me?

Have fun, don't take yourself too seriously

The most important thing to remember about tea leaf reading is to enjoy yourself. Relaxing with friends over a pot of tea and some cookies is one of life's greatest pleasures.

"You can never get a cup of tea large enough, or a book long enough to suit me."

C.S. Lewis

3
All About Tea

The history of tea

The Chinese have consumed tea for thousands of years dating back to at least 3000 BC. The Chinese recognized the medicinal benefits of tea long before anyone had ever heard of antioxidents.

By at least 1000 BC, Chinese physicians recognized tea's ability to improve not only physical health but mental functioning as well. And by 100 BC tea was firmly established as not only a medicine but as an important part of the Chinese diet.

Myths about tea

There are many myths about tea, its origin and cultivation. In one legend describing the origin of tea cultivation, it was said that the Buddha accidentally fell asleep while meditating. When he woke up he was so disgusted at his weakness that to prevent this from happening again he cut off his own eyelids, they fell to the ground where they took root and grew into the first tea bushes.

In one popular Chinese legend about the origin of tea drinking, the Emperor of China was said to have been drinking a bowl of hot water when a few leaves blew off a nearby tree into his bowl, changing the colour. The Emperor took a sip of the coloured water and was pleased with its flavour. The legend goes on to say that the emperor then discovered the medicinal properties of various herbs by chewing the leaves, stems, and roots of various plants. If he discovered a poisonous plant, he would chew tea leaves as an antidote to the poison.

There is even a myth regarding the harvesting of tea by monkeys. It is said that the farmers would chase monkeys up into tea trees and then stand under tea trees and taunt the monkeys. The monkeys would get angry, and throw handfuls of tea leaves at the farmers. An entertaining story, but unlikely since tea grows on bushes not trees.

Tea in Japan

Sometime around 700 AD, tea was introduced to Japan by Buddhist monks. Although Japan is well known for its love of tea, oddly, there is very little recorded history regarding divination by tea leaf reading in Japan.

Tea arrives in the west

During the 16th and 17th centuries Holland was a great trading power and the first shipments of tea from China arrived in Holland in 1609. Tea did not reach Great Britain until 1650, at which time it was heavily taxed and very expensive and therefore a luxury available only to the wealthy.

Tea incites rebellion

The British government passed a law forcing the British colonies to buy their tea only from Britain so that the British government could receive the revenues from the tea tax. The Boston Tea Party on Dec. 16. 1773, which was a revolt against paying taxes to a government where they had no elected representation, was a key event in the growth of the American Revolution

Tea became more affordable for common people in Britain after 1784 when the tax on tea was dramatically reduced. From that time until the early 20th century, tea leaf reading was a very common method of divination used by women in Britain and throughout the British colonies. Everyone had at least one family member who read tea leaves.

A guide to the different types of tea

North Americans are not as passionate about their tea as the British. I think this is because most of us have never really experienced a good cup of tea. The insipid blend of low-grade tea found in most of the generic tea bags available in our grocery stores, combined with attempting to brew tea with lukewarm water, results in a rather uninspiring drink. But it doesn't have to be like this. There is a whole world of tea for us to explore, and almost all of them can be used for divination purposes.

What exactly is tea?

Many people think of tea as a drink made by steeping an herb in hot water. But "real" tea is created by brewing the dried and cured leaves of a specific evergreen bush, known as Camellia Sinensis, in boiling water. Camellia Sinensis is a plant native to China that has been perfected over many centuries and transplanted to many regions of the world.

Most of the world's tea crop is grown in China, India, Sri Lanka, and Japan. Teas from each of these areas taste very different. The altitude at which it is grown, the soil, the climate, and the way the tea is processed all have an effect on the flavour. The highest quality teas are grown at high altitudes. The high altitude causes it to mature more slowly with a lower yield, resulting in a more expensive product.

Harvesting and processing tea

Tea "flushes" (the terminal bud and 2 young leaves), are plucked from Camellia Sinensis bushes twice a year during spring and summer. However, in some areas where the climate permits, autumn or winter harvests are also possible. Picking is generally done by hand because it is difficult to harvest by machine on the mountain slopes where tea is often grown. The tea is picked with a quick snap of the wrist to prevent twisting or pinching it, which would reduce the quality of the leaves. Poorer quality teas are sometimes picked by machine, resulting in more broken leaves and twigs in the mix.

Tea leaves begin to wilt soon after picking. Wilting removes excess water from the leaves. The leaves are usually stacked in a breezy room while they wilt. The leaves lose much of their weight in water during wilting.

Once they have wilted sufficiently the leaves are sometimes bruised by being kneaded or rolled-over by heavy wheels. This releases some of the leaf juices, which aids in the oxidation process and changes the taste of the tea.

If the tea requires oxidation (referred to as fermentation in the tea industry), the leaves are left on their own in a closed room to darken.

The tea is then heated to stop the oxidation at a desired level.

The damp tea leaves are then kneaded by hand or machine to form strips. The strips can then be formed into other shapes, such as spirals, pellets, balls and other elaborate shapes.

Finally, drying is done to prepare the tea for shipping and sale. Baking is the most common method of drying.

There are over 3000 varieties of teas, but most fall into three main categories: black, oolong and green. Tea falls into one of these 3 categories according to the degree of processing or "fermentation" the leaves have undergone.

Black Tea

Black tea is the most common form of tea, and until recently was pretty much the only tea available to us in grocery stores in North America. The Chinese call this type of tea red tea because when brewed the resulting tea liquid produced is an amber/red colour. In the western world it is called black tea because the dried tea leaves used to brew it appear black.

You will often see the words "Orange Pekoe" on a package of tea. Many people mistakenly think that this is a type of tea but actually it is simply a grading system that is used to rate the quality of the dried leaves.

Black tea requires more processing than green or oolong tea. The processing time takes between two weeks and one month. The harvested leaves sit on shelves to wilt for a period of time before the oxidation process begins. When the leaves have wilted long enough they are placed in a humidity-controlled room to allow them to oxidize. Oxidation causes the leaves to darken and results in an increase in the caffeine content.

After the oxidation/fermentation process is complete, the leaves are heated and dried to stop the fermentation process. For some varieties of tea the leaves are chopped into small pieces to speed up the drying process.

Black Tea

Post-fermented (Pu-erh) tea

Pu-erh tea should really be in a category all its own. It is a type of Chinese black tea usually consumed for medicinal purposes rather than for pleasure. It is different from other black teas because it is oxidized/fermented twice and then it is left for a period of time to allow it to mature. During this maturation process a layer of mould develops on the leaves. The mould is what gives it its medicinal value but also gives it its distinctive "medicinal" flavour that most people find unpleasant.

Green Tea

Green tea retains the original green colour of the tea leaves because it is not fermented during processing. Brewing green tea produces a pale green-yellow coloured liquid with a grassy flavour closer to the original flavour of the leaf.

Green tea used to make up approximately ten percent of the world's tea, but this percentage is increasing because of the increased awareness of its health benefits.

All Japanese teas are green. Chinese green teas are most familiar to us in the west as the tea served in Chinese restaurants.

The production process involves stacking the leaves on shelves to allow them to wither, then heating them to prevent fermentation. The leaves are then rolled and dried.

Oolong Tea (sometimes called pouchong)

Oolong tea lies somewhere in the middle between green and black tea. It is fermented like black tea, but the process is stopped part way through when the leaves are a red-brown colour.

The fermentation process is stopped at exactly the right time in order to produce a balance in taste between black tea and green tea. Having grown up drinking copious amounts of black tea, I find that drinking green tea tastes a little too much like chewing on stalks of grass for my taste. For me, oolong tea is a good compromise.

White Tea

White tea is the least processed tea variety. It does not go through the withering or fermentation process. This rare and very expensive tea is produced primarily in China.

It is sometimes called Silvertip Pekoe or White Needle, because it is made up of the white new-growth buds of the tea plant that have been shielded from sunlight to prevent the formation of chlorophyll. The buds are picked at dawn and dried naturally.

When brewed, the tea is a pale yellow straw colour with a slightly sweet or nutty flavour.

Kukicha

Kukicha (sometimes referred to as "winter tea") is a Japanese tea made from twigs and old leaves picked from the tea plant during its dormant season and dried over a fire. It is consumed as a health food in Japan.

Rooibos or Red Tea

Rooibos, sometimes referred to as Red Tea, is not really tea at all because it does not come from the Camellia Sinensis plant. It is an herbal plant that grows in South Africa I am mentioning it here because it has become a very popular caffeine-free alternative to tea.

Rooiboos/Red Tea

Blended Teas

In order to achieve flavour consistency from one season to the next, most packages of commercial tea are made up of a blend of teas from different areas.

Some of the traditional blended teas that you might be familiar with include English Breakfast Tea, Earl Grey Tea and Russian Caravan Tea.

English Breakfast Tea is a blend of Indian teas.

Earl Grey Tea is a blend of Chinese teas flavoured with bergamot oil giving it its distinctive perfumey taste and smell. A gift of this tea was given to the 2nd Earl Grey (the British Prime Minister in the 1830's) by a Chinese diplomat.

Russian Caravan Tea is a blend of teas from China. It was originally transported to Europe through Russia via camel caravan. The long cold trip through Russia was believed to give the tea its distinct flavour, different from that of teas that reached Europe through the warmer southerly route through India. But the distinctive taste is probably more due to the addition of Lapsang Souchong tea to the blend. Lapsang Souchong tea has a distinctive smoky flavour that was originally added as a preservative.

Flavoured Teas

Because of its naturally mild flavour, tea easily absorbs other aromas and tastes. Tea can be flavoured naturally with dried fruit, flowers and spices, or it can be flavoured artificially with just about any flavour imaginable.

The Chinese are known for their flower flavoured teas such as jasmine, orchid, rose, and magnolia, but they have also brewed tea with onions, orange peel, peach leaves, and berries for centuries.

In Arab countries mint is the preferred flavouring.

In India, spicy "masala tea" is made by boiling black tea and spices such as cardamom, cinnamon, ginger, cloves, and pepper; in milk rather than water. It is usually served heavily sweetened with sugar.

Herbal Infusions and Tisanes

The word "tea" is often used to describe any drink created by boiling the leaves of a plant. But since technically speaking, true "tea" is only made from the leaves of the Camellia Sinensis plant, any other leaf-derived drinks should be referred to as tisanes or herbal infusions.

Ginger root tea, Kava root tea and licorice teas are examples of herbal infusions made from roots.

While tea leaves are the traditional choice, any beverage that leaves sediment in the cup can be used for divination.

"Tea is liquid wisdom."

Anonymous

4
Tea Leaf Reading in 10 Steps

Here is an easy 10-step method to get you started reading tea leaves immediately.

Step 1: Assemble your tools

You will need:

- Boiling water
- Loose tea
- A tea spoon
- A tea cup and saucer with a white or light colored interior
- A tea pot (if making more than one cup of tea)
- Milk, sugar, lemons, honey, whatever you use in your tea
- Cookies or tea biscuits are always a nice touch
- A paper and pen to write down what you see
- Paper towels or napkins to catch any drips (very useful for discretely spitting out tea leaves)

To make a good cup of tea the water should be boiling when it hits the tea. Most of the time in restaurants the tea is made with hot water from the coffee machine, YUCK!

Boiling water is particularly important when you are using loose tea leaves which are not finely ground like tea bags. It takes longer for tea leaves to steep than it does for the tea bags that we are accustomed to.

Silk tea bags were invented around 1900, and the rectangular paper tea bags that we are familiar with were invented in the 1940's. It wasn't until televisions became common in peoples homes in the 1950's that tea bags really took off because people appreciated being able to brew a quick cup of tea during commercials.

Step 2: Make a cup of tea

Bring the water to a boil. For one cup of tea place 1 teaspoonful of loose tea in a white or light colored teacup. Pour in the boiling water. Let the tea steep for a few minutes.

If you are reading for more than just yourself, make a pot of tea. Warm the teapot by pouring in some of the boiling water, swish it around and pour out the water. Add 1 heaping teaspoon of tea for each cup of tea that you will be making, then pour in the boiling water. Cover with a tea cozy or a towel and leave the tea to steep for a few minutes. How long you leave the tea steeping is a matter of personal preference. Most people in North America prefer their tea weak, while the British prefer it stronger.

Remove the tea cozy. Open the tea pot lid for a moment and give the tea a stir with a spoon. Pour each person's tea into their cup without using a tea strainer, allowing tea leaves to flow freely into each cup.

Look into each cup to check for the presence of bubbles (which represent a celebration) or for tea leaves floating on the surface (which indicate that the inquirer will be coming into some money)

Step 3: Fix your tea the way you like it

Tea is to be enjoyed, it is not medicine that must be endured, so fix it the way you like it. Personally, I prefer it strong, sweet, and with lots of milk (or better still cream), but you can have it black, with milk, with lemon, with honey, whatever you prefer.

Step 4: Sip your tea while you focus on what you want to know

Once your tea is the perfect temperature for you, begin drinking it. Some leaves may be floating, but most will have sunk to the bottom of the cup. Sip the tea so that you can avoid getting too many of the tea leaves in your mouth, they won't hurt you, but having tea leaves in your mouth spoils the tea drinking experience a bit, and besides you want to leave plenty of leaves in the cup.

Enjoy your tea. Being happy and relaxed is the most important step in reading tea leaves. As you relax, identify the issue foremost in your mind. Focus on that thought. If nothing specific comes to mind, that is fine, the tea leaves will still have a message for you. Focus on enjoying the tea and enjoying the company if you are with friends.

Step 5: Leave a small amount of tea at the bottom of your cup.

Drink down to the bottom of your cup but leave just enough that the tea leaves can swish around freely. It doesn't require much fluid, no more than about ½ an inch.

Step 6: Swirl three times and turn the tea cup over onto its saucer

Hold your nearly empty tea cup in your hand and disperse the tea leaves around the interior of the cup by giving it three good swirls. There are differences of opinion about which direction you should swirl the cup. I do it in a counter-clockwise direction because that is what feels right to me. I don't think the direction matters, the important thing is that you do it in the same direction consistently as part of your tea leaf reading ritual.

Pour out the small amount of remaining tea by turning your tea cup over onto its saucer.

Wait three seconds to allow the tea to drain out before turning the cup back over.

Step 7: Identify the symbols

Look into the cup. What is the first symbol you see anywhere in the cup? This is the dominant theme of the reading. If at first you don't see anything, relax, squint your eyes, and allow your imagination to run free and something will pop into view. Get out your piece of paper and pen and start writing down the symbols as you see them.

After you have identified the first image, start at the handle and read the images clockwise from the rim in a spiral down towards the bottom of the cup. Imagine that the cup is divided into three sections: the rim, the middle and the base. The rim area is the area above the water line when you first poured the tea. The middle section is the area between the rim and bottom. The base is the bottom of the cup up to the level of tea that was left in the cup before you tipped out the excess tea.

Make a note of each symbol, where it is located and if it is next to another symbol. Look for letters and numbers, these can be especially significant. Take your time.

Step 8: Interpret the meaning of the symbols

What is the thought that immediately pops into your mind when you see each symbol? What does each image mean to you? You are the person best qualified to read your own cup. If you are reading someone else's cup, just trust that the universe, God, your higher power, your super-conscious mind, or whatever you choose to call it, has put the images there and will give you the information/understanding that you need to interpret them.

Evaluate the timing of the symbols. The span of time represented by a tea cup reading rarely exceeds 12 months. It is possible to have the reading represent the next 12 weeks, 12 days, or even 12 hours.

The closer an image is to the top of the cup the sooner it will take place, while the closer it is to the bottom the farther away it is in time. The images in the rim area usually represent the present time. Closer to the bottom refers to events or influences a little farther away. The base of the cup represents the future, or the outcome of a situation.

Step 9: Read the saucer

When you are finished with the cup, have a look at the saucer. Did any of the tea leaves end up in the saucer when you turned over the tea cup? If not, then the message in the cup is all there is to the message. But if there are tea leaves sitting in the saucer you can try to read the saucer to see if it can add to your understanding of the message.

Begin by swirling the liquid around three times like you did with the cup, and then pour the liquid down the sink (or out onto the grass if you are having a tea party out in the back yard).

Since the saucer has no handle to use to start reading from, in this case start from the place where you poured off the tea, you should be able to see the spot where the liquid flowed leaving a trail of tea leaves in its wake. Hold the saucer in your hand with the pouring spot at the 12 o'clock position. Read the images in a clockwise spiral from the outer edge of the saucer down to the point in the middle.

Step 10: Remember to have fun!

Don't take yourself too seriously. The best messages come when you are having fun, don't be afraid to get a little silly.

If at first you don't see anything then make something up! I know that this sounds like I'm telling you to fake the reading, but it works. Doing this seems to take the pressure off, it tells your internal censor to go take a break, and will open up the floodgates and let the real message flow.

Summary of the 10 simple steps to reading tea leaves

Step 1: Assemble your tools

Step 2: Make a cup of tea

Step 3: Fix your tea the way you like it

Step 4: Sip your tea while you focus on what you want to know

Step 5: Leave a small amount of tea at the bottom of your cup

Step 6: Swirl three times and turn the tea cup over onto its saucer

Step 7: Identify the symbols

Step 8: Interpret the meaning of the symbols

Step 9: Read the saucer

Step 10: Remember to have fun!

5

Tea Leaf Reading as a Business

As you become more proficient at reading for friends and family it is only natural that other people will start asking you to read for them. This is a delicate situation. At what point does it become a business?

People really want and need the advice, and if you are really good you are providing a valuable service, and it can be a rewarding way of earning a living, but there are legal issues and ethical issues to consider before you take that step.

Is it legal where you live?

I am not really able to address the legal issues because I am not a lawyer, and the rules are so different depending on where you are located.

Your best bet is to call the municipality where you live (the town or city, the county etc.) and ask whether there are bylaws regarding psychics. Ask them if you need a business license. Generally speaking if tarot readers and palm readers have set up shop where you are then tea leaf readers are probably classified into that category of business.

One other consideration is that since you are providing tea to your client you might have to deal with health department regulations regarding the way you prepare the tea and wash the tea cups, but your municipal office should be able to direct you to the person you need to speak to regarding that.

Insurance coverage?

If you are operating out of your home you need to talk to your property insurance company to ensure that you are covered for liability insurance in the event that someone was to fall and hurt themselves. Many homeowner or tenant policies will not cover you if you start operating a business out of your home.

Some people have successfully gotten around the liability issue by operating out of a local coffee shop or metaphysical bookstore that already has liability insurance in place.

Malpractice insurance

Another issue is malpractice insurance. What if you tell a client something that upsets them, or they end up doing something stupid as a result of your reading and afterward they decide to sue you?

Therapists, doctors, lawyers, accountants, hairdressers and other professionals can buy malpractice insurance, but I am not aware of any insurance companies that provide malpractice insurance for psychics. Your best bet is to call around to various insurance companies and see if they know where you could get this kind of coverage.

Disturbing developments in Britain

Apparently, in some parts of the United States if you are an ordained minister you are allowed to do psychic or mediumistic readings and are protected from liability because it is considered pastoral counseling, but this isn't enough to protect you in Britain. In 2008 Britain replaced the Fraudulent Mediums Act (which was passed in 1951) with new Consumer Protection regulations that force psychics and mediums to issue disclaimers such as "this is a scientific experiment, the results of which cannot be guaranteed" before they read for a client.

A step backward in time

For psychics, the passing of Britain's new Consumer Protection regulations is a step backward. Under the legislation that they replace, the Fraudulent Mediums Act, prosecutors had to prove fraud and dishonest intent to secure a criminal conviction, but now the onus is on the psychic to prove that they did not mislead, coerce or take advantage of any "vulnerable" consumers. But how can you prove that you did not do something?

If this sort of legislation can become law in Britain which has more than 300 Spiritualist Churches, and where in the past almost everyone had a Granny or an Aunt that read tea leaves, it can happen anywhere.

20th century witch hunt

The last person to be jailed in Britain under the previous Witchcraft Act of 1735 was a Scottish medium,

Helen Duncan, who was convicted and spent 9 months in jail in 1944.

Witnesses testified that at a group demonstration in Portsmouth, England Mrs. Duncan contacted the spirit of a sailor who had drowned on the HMS Barham. This was particularly evidential since military authorities had not yet released the information that the Barham had sunk.

Many people familiar with the case believe that she was imprisoned because she was so good that the government was afraid that she would inadvertently reveal the secret D-Day plans. Under other circumstances a person charged with this crime would have received a fine, but Helen Duncan was given a prison sentence that coincidentally extended until after D-Day and the final assault into Germany that effectively ended WW2.

As a child I remember my mother telling me about how she and my grandmother had gone to see Helen Duncan for a reading in Edinburgh, Scotland during the Second World War. They had gone to various mediums and Spiritualist meetings hoping to get information about the fate of my uncle whose merchant marine ship disappeared without a trace at the start of the war.

Obviously, they were hoping to hear that my uncle was still alive and well, possibly being held as a prisoner of war somewhere, but instead, Mrs. Duncan informed them that the ship had been sunk and all the crew on board, including my uncle, were drowned. She gave them some other personal information that convinced my mother of her accuracy and her sincerity. It wasn't until years after the war that Helen

Duncan's accuracy was confirmed for my family when the government released the official report regarding the fate of these merchant marine seamen.

So that there is no misunderstanding, I want to point out that Helen Duncan was a medium, not a tea leaf reader, although I'm quite sure that she was able to read tea leaves since it was very common in Scotland at that time. She was one of history's greatest physical mediums, which means that she was able to go into a trance and the spirits of people who had passed on were able to materialize and be seen by witnesses in the room, which is an extremely rare skill entirely different from what I am talking about in this book.

The reason that I am mentioning Helen Duncan's story is to point out that, particularly involving things of this nature which people don't completely understand, being very good at something will not necessarily protect you from problems. In fact, it was because she was so good that she wound up in jail.

Lawsuits and other legal headaches

I really struggled with whether or not to include a discussion of negative things like lawsuits or criminal charges in this book. You see, I really believe that what you focus on grows, or in this case, what you expect to have happen will eventually happen. By thinking about, talking about, and taking steps to protect yourself against something, you are increasing the likelihood that the event will actually take place.

On the other hand, it would be very foolish to pretend

that these things don't ever happen, so I am including a discussion about protecting yourself from legal problems.

I think that the best way to protect yourself is to ensure that you are totally honest and ethical in your dealings with everyone. Since we tend to attract to ourselves people (and in this case clients) who have similar vibrations or similar energy as ours, if we are honest and sincere we will tend to attract clients who are also honest and sincere.

Asking clients to sign a release

Some readers ask clients to sign a release before reading for them. This is a good idea, but it would also be a good idea to get a lawyer to look at your release to ensure that it is worded in a way that will actually protect you in the community where you operate.

Keep an audio recording of your sessions

Keeping a recording of the session is one of the best methods of protecting yourself.

Record the session onto your computer, give a CD to your client or email them an MP3 file and keep a copy for yourself. Doing this has many benefits:

1) Clients love it and feel that they have gotten good value for their money because they can listen to it over again later.

2) If you give out a CD it is good advertising because if you have a printed label with your name

and phone number on it the client is unlikely to loose your contact information.

3) It reminds you to be careful with what you say (something that is good to practice regardless of whether or not you are being recorded).

4) It is proof that you can use in court to deny any false claims against you.

5) Just knowing that you keep a recording of what you said is enough to discourage frivolous lawsuits from scam artists who might otherwise consider you an easy mark.

Some readers still use audio tapes to record their sessions for their clients, but this is a problem because it does not provide you with a copy very easily, and most clients no longer have tape players.

Another possibility is that you can write out the symbols that you see, along with your interpretation of them on a piece of paper and photocopy it to give to your client and keep the original in your file, but this requires that you have access to a photo copier.

Privacy laws and your client files

Many countries have privacy laws in place to protect an individual's personal information. If you keep any kind of information about a client, such as recordings of the readings, your notes, or the client's contact information you must be very careful how you handle this information. Many psychologists and therapists keep their files confidential by coding the information in such a way that anyone snooping through the files would not be able to tell whose file it was.

Other than signed releases, I think it is probably better not to keep files with personal information about client readings. Obviously you will definitely want to ask your clients if you can put them on your email mailing list so that you can send out a newsletter or email marketing from time to time, but other than their email address you would not have any identifying information about them.

If you take credit cards, talk to the merchant services people who handle your account and ask them how you should handle the credit card numbers once you have put through a transaction. They will tell you how long you need to keep the record of the transaction and how to handle disposing of those records.

Limit how often you will read for a client

Some people are very needy, and can become dependent on you for advice, or even just for someone to talk to. For this reason it is best if you put limits on how often you will read for any one client. Some people limit clients to once a year, others are willing to read for clients monthly; you decide what is right for you, but whatever time limit you choose be sure to stick to it.

I know it is tempting to agree to see them more often, because they seem to really NEED you (and let's face it that is very good for our egos), and you could probably find a use for the money, but don't fall into that trap. We are not helping clients when we allow them to become dependent on us. Our lives are meant to be lived, and that includes making our own decisions and living with the consequences. A little bit of guidance from the other side is fine, but we are on this earth for an adventure, and part of that adventure involves not always knowing in advance what is going to happen.

Besides, limiting how often you will read for a client is the best way to prove that you are not "taking advantage of vulnerable clients."

Charging for your services

Money is energy, and every time that you read for someone there should be an exchange of energy. When you read for friends and family it isn't always necessary to charge money because you are always exchanging energy with these people, or at least you should be, in the form of love, thoughtful gestures, help, gifts, etc.

For clients it is important that you expect them to give you something in exchange, even if, because of the laws where you live, you do not have a set rate, but rather accept gifts (donations), it is important that they recognize the value of what you are giving them in return.

Money is the best way to measure value because people in our society value what they pay for. In fact, the more you charge the more people tend to appreciate your service, and the more likely they are to actually listen to what you have to say.

Also, the more you charge, the more you value yourself,

and the more you value yourself, the better you will become. I realize that this is somewhat circular reasoning, but it works, and I am convinced that it is part of why psychics or mediums who charge astronomical amounts of money tend to be busier than the ones who charge $10 a reading.

I know that it could be argued that the really good ones charge more because they are so good that they get very busy and have to put their prices up, but this is not what I have witnessed, in my experience people tend to develop their skill to match their prices. This is not to say that I haven't had some absolutely brilliant $5-$10 readings, and some dreadful $100 ones.

How much should you charge?

You have to decide the rate that feels comfortable for you. Find out what the going rate is for tarot readings, palm readings and other psychic readings in your area and make your decision accordingly. Unfortunately, tea leaf readings are generally not as expensive as other types of psychic readings.

Dealing with skeptics

Don't waste your time trying to convince a skeptic. You can never convince a skeptic that this is real. If someone is convinced that this is impossible and you give a wonderfully accurate reading they will assume that you got the information fraudulently, and if your reading is anything less than perfect (and it is never 100% accurate) anything that you misinterpret will be proof to them that it doesn't work. Either way you can't win.

There are lots of people out there who go around to psychics and mediums trying to prove that they are frauds, and let's face it, there are plenty of frauds out there. Just be totally honest and ethical, and if you don't like the energy of a particular client just refuse to read for them. Explain that it isn't going to work and refuse to take their money.

There is a huge demand for your services because everyone wants to have their fortune told, everyone wants to know what is going to happen down the road. Even skeptics would love to be astounded by a reader who can give them a really good reading.

Building your business

You can't build a business if no one knows about you. This is the dilemma that many people, especially women, struggle with. You want to read for people, and you believe in what you are doing, but you are embarrassed about promoting yourself or perhaps you are afraid of drawing the attention of the "religious right."

Well make your decision one way or the other, because in this business you cannot straddle the fence. If you are afraid of the nut cases you can be sure that they will find you, so you might as well make it easy for the legitimate clients to find you as well.

The fastest way to build your business is to get business cards and give them out like candy at Halloween. The cards don't have to be fancy, in fact simple is better, make sure they say who you are and what you do and how to reach you, don't bother with fancy logos and slogans. It always amazes me how many business cards I get that have a fancy business name and yet I can't remember who gave it to me or what kind of business it is. Just go ahead and get cheap ones so you won't be reluctant to give them out by the handful. Give a bunch to everyone you know and ask them to hand them out for you. Tack a few up on every bulletin board that you can find.

Most of your clients, at least initially, will be women, so hairdressers are great places to leave a bunch of your cards. Offer to do readings at the beauty salon (they often provide tea and coffee for clients so reading tea leaves can fit right in). Bookstores and coffee shops are two other great places to do readings. Offer to give the store a percentage of the money you bring in and it can be a money maker for both of you.

Obviously, word of mouth is your best advertising, but you need those first few satisfied clients before the word of mouth can spread. If you are good, in time you will be so busy that you will have trouble keeping up.

There is no competition

It doesn't matter how many other psychic readers there are in your area, because really there is no such thing as competition. Your clients will come to you, and if they choose another reader they weren't your clients to begin with. In fact, the more readers there are in a particular area the better, because the people in your area will be familiar with the concept of paying for a reading.

If you believe in the concept of scarcity and competition you will always be struggling for money because that is what you will continually see around you. It is important to recognize scarcity for the lie that it is, and keep reminding yourself that there is plenty of business to go around.

As a reader who has developed your skill enough to read for others you already know that this skill comes from a power outside of yourself. Call it the universal intelligence, call it God, call it whatever you want, just remember that this power can send you all the clients who are right for you.

Focus on what you want, and ignore what you don't want.

Where will you see clients?

Many readers see clients at home, while others prefer to keep strangers out of their house and away from their families.

There are several advantages to working at home:

- You will have lower overhead and therefore be able to keep more of the money as profit

- If you work at home and make a profit some of your household expenses might become tax deductions (talk to an accountant)

- If someone fails to show up for their appointment you can just keep doing what you would otherwise be doing at home

- You don't waste time and money commuting

Obviously there are disadvantages as well:

- Your family could be exposed to some people that you otherwise might not want them exposed to

- If you have kids at home the noise can make it difficult to concentrate on the messages

- It can be hard to get away from work because your clients will always know where to find you

Home parties

Home parties can be very profitable. The way it usually works is that the hostess will invite you to her home to read for her guests. Generally, the host will pay you a flat rate for the evening and you will read for everyone present. Basically you are the entertainment for the evening, so they are expecting you to be fun and entertaining and give everyone a good time. If the idea of giving readings as entertainment offends you then obviously this type of party is not for you.

The other possibility is that the host will invite to the event but will not pay you. In this case you will be paid a small amount or a donation by each guest that chooses to have a reading. In this case usually the host will set aside a relatively private spot so that each reading can be more confidential.

How you feel about doing readings for people who have been drinking will also affect whether doing home parties works for you.

Another possibility is that the host treats this similar to

a Tupperware™ party where they invite everyone they know and it is expected that the guests will "buy" something, in this case a reading, and in exchange you give the host a percentage of the revenue, and a free reading.

One of the big advantages of doing parties is that you meet potential clients, give out a ton of business cards, and if they like you they will come to see you for another reading in the future and refer their friends to you. If you are good you can build up a very large client base from doing parties.

Coffee shops, restaurants, book stores, and bars

As I mentioned earlier, you can often make a deal with businesses to let you work out of their business location. This can be beneficial to both of you. You will get business that you wouldn't otherwise have gotten, and the host business benefits by being able to offer an additional service to their customers and generate some additional revenue.

Obviously, tea leaf reading does not lend itself to doing on-line or telephone readings.

Psychic fairs

I once had a very good tea leaf reading at an indoor psychic fair. The reader obviously had thought this through very carefully and came equipped to handle lots of clients. She brought along:

- a very professional looking sign on a small tripod
- an electric kettle
- 4 folding chairs

- 2 little folding tables
- 2 plastic tablecloths
- a numbered sign-up sheet
- a credit card imprinter
- disposable paper coffee cups with little handles
- small disposable plates
- regular tea bags
- a pair of scissors to cut open the tea bags
- artificial creamers (no refrigeration needed)
- lemon juice
- packets of sugar
- stir sticks
- napkins
- garbage bags
- 2 square plastic pails with lids

All of the loose items fit tightly in the 2 square plastic pails, and everything (including the tables and the chairs fit neatly onto a small dolly that she used to transport her supplies to and from her car, and which stowed away conveniently under one of the tables during the fair. Most importantly she also brought along her teenaged granddaughter as her assistant.

In her booth she set up an area at the back corner where she did the actual readings, it consisted of a chair for herself and the client along with a small table which held some business cards and advertising material. (In this case she was not asking clients to sign a release form, but if she had one this table would have been a good spot for that.) On this table is where she had the small disposable plates, and underneath the table was were she kept the plastic pail where she dumped out the excess tea from the bottom of the cups.

At the front of her booth was a table containing her sign, a sign-up sheet, the electric kettle, the disposable cups, the tea and fixings, a pail with a garbage bag in it.

Her assistant would run back and forth from the bathroom filling the kettle with water and boiling it. As each client arrived at the booth the assistant would explain the routine, get them to sign up on the sign-up sheet, take the cash or process the credit card, and fix their tea. The clients would then sit at the waiting area chairs, sip their tea, and wait for their turn.

Once each client finished their tea and moved over to the client chair the reader would give them one of the small plates to use as a saucer and then dump the excess tea in the pail. Every hour or so the assistant would take the pail over to the bathrooms to dump it.

Back of booth

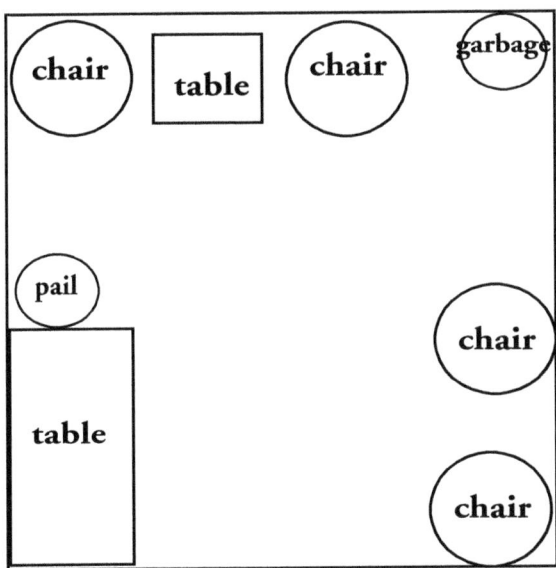

Front of booth

Personally, I do not like the idea of using tea from tea bags because it is too fine and doesn't make really clear images, more of a sludge. Also it doesn't make for the nicest tea drinking experience because it his hard to keep the bits of tea out of your mouth. I suspect that she had probably just run out of loose tea (or perhaps the tea bags were just cheaper). Regardless, this reader was very good at giving readings and was able to handle at least 6 clients per hour, or about 50 clients over the course of the day. It must have been exhausting for her, but an excellent day's revenue and a great way of building up her clientele.

Outdoor fairs and street festivals

I had an excellent tea leaf reading at a local county fair. In this case the reader had a small travel trailer that she used for her readings. She had a table and chairs outside under an awning where you could drink your tea and wait for your turn. In this case she used loose tea and Styrofoam cups. Obviously these cups didn't have a handle, but she simply drew a line where the tea cup handle would normally be, and told you to hold it in your dominant hand and have the line facing your knuckles while you drank it. When it was your turn the reader brought you into the trailer where you sat at the table for the reading.

This worked well for her because she had water, a stove and a fridge to keep milk for the tea. She also had her own accommodations while she was on the road. She earned her living doing readings like this, moving along from fair to fair.

While this type of nomadic lifestyle does not work for most people, you could still do occassional outdoor fairs if you have access to electricity to boil water and set yourself up with a table and an umbrella.

Keep everything legal

Many people are tempted to try and hide the income they receive from doing readings and not declare it on their income tax return. Don't do it, it is not worth it for many reasons.

The obvious reason is that the penalties for tax evasion are stiff no matter where you live. In order to evade taxes successfully you would have to leave no paper trail. That means that you couldn't put the money in your bank account, you couldn't use it to pay your normal bills. You would only be able to accept cash, no checks, no credit cards, and you could only spend that cash on untraceable things like groceries and gasoline. What is the point? Even then, you would always be vulnerable to someone reporting you, someone with a grudge against you, or a jealous competitor. You would always be looking over your shoulder.

Sure, nobody likes to hand over their money to the government, but really, the tax burden for a self-employed person is not so bad. There are plenty of legitimate tax deductions that self-employed people can use to reduce the amount of taxes they owe. Talk to an accountant and hang on to your receipts.

But there is another reason for being honest and reporting the income. By not wanting to pay the taxes you are telling yourself and the universe that you don't feel that you have enough money, that you do not feel abundant, and since what you give out is what you get back, you will always be exactly what you claim to be, in this case without enough money and not abundant. By not trusting that you will always have plenty of money to pay your taxes you effectively block the flow of money coming to you.

I discuss this concept in more detail in my book **"The Spirituality of Money"** ISBN 978-0-9783939-3-9

6

Meditation

Focusing your mind through meditation

Learning to focus your mind through meditation is an important step in developing your psychic ability. Meditation develops your mind the way weight lifting develops your body, and like weight lifting it is a gradual process. No one expects to be able to lift heavy weights the first time they try it, so you shouldn't expect to be able to keep your mind focused for long periods of time initially either.

Our minds are always active. We are constantly thinking about something whether we realize it or not. Many people are under the mistaken impression that meditation involves training yourself to think about nothing, and are frustrated when they find it impossible to do. The minute you sit down and attempt to think about nothing you find a million random thoughts coming to your attention. "Did I remember to lock the car?" "What should I make for dinner?" It seems that your mind uses this pause to bring to your attention every imaginable thought.

What do you need for meditation?

While it might be nice to have a room in your home dedicated to meditation, most of us do not have this luxury, and besides, it is not necessary. In fact, it is better if you can learn to meditate anywhere in any situation.

It is best to meditate in a well lighted room. This helps to keep you from drifting off to sleep. You can meditate with your eyes fully open, half open, or slightly open, letting in just two small slits of light. It is a little more difficult to learn to mediate with your eyes open because of the additional sensory input from your vision, your attention tends to get caught by the things you see around you.

Meditating with your eyes fully closed is fine as long as the room remains brightly lit, so that enough light passes through the eyelids to keep your brain alert. When attempting to meditate in a darkened room your brain interprets this as a signal to start shutting itself down for sleep. Sleep inducing hormones are released and your heart rate and circulation are reduced. You gently drift away. While this is a pleasant experience it is not meditation. Meditation means that you are relaxed as if sleeping, but your consciousness is fully awake.

Music or silence?

There is a difference of opinion about whether or not music assists in your meditation. Some traditionalists say that music is another form of distraction for your mind and by playing music you are not really training your mind to focus out distractions, but are putting yourself into a self-hypnotic state.

While it is probably best if you can develop the ability to meditate without music so that you can meditate anywhere at any time if you are in a stressful situation and need to for relaxation purposes, there are advantages of meditating to music.

- The very act of putting on a meditation music CD can be a cue to tell your mind that you are about to meditate.

- A meditation music CD can serve as a timer so that you are not distracted wondering how long you have been sitting.

Music can be nice but it is not necessary. Personally I meditate both ways since they both have their advantages.

Meditation posture

The most important thing is to be comfortable. Some people are able to sit cross legged on the floor quite comfortably. I am not one of them. I prefer to sit upright in a chair, or slightly reclining with my feet elevated. Many mediation teachers tell you that your spine must be straight and completely vertical but this is difficult for many people to do for long periods. I think that as long as you are sitting comfortably with your spine relatively straight it is not necessary to be sitting rigidly upright.

It is believed that energy rises up your spinal column during a meditation session. Think of this energy as being like water in a garden hose, if you gently bend the hose into a mild arc, the flow of water will not be affected, but if you bend it over and kink the hose the flow of water will be cut off. So sit comfortably but don't cut off the flow of energy.

To send energy out into another person, such as when practicing Reiki, the feet are planted firmly on the floor and the palms of the hands are open thereby creating a clear conduit through which the energy can flow. But for meditation purposes you want to form a continuous loop circuit so that the energy created builds up and remains in the body. This can be done by touching your feet together or by forming a loop with your thumb and middle finger.

What do you do while sitting?

The traditional eastern approach to meditation is to relax, let go, and do nothing. Be consciously in the moment and watch yourself as a silent witness. Be aware of your breathing and your heart beat. If thoughts come to mind, simply observe the thoughts but do not add to them by your active participation. Be a detached and passive observer and feel your connection to the universe. This is called ***mindfulness meditation***. It sounds simple but it is actually very difficult for most people to master.

There is another form of meditation that is easier to master. It is called ***concentration meditation.*** In this type of meditation you focus on one particular object or thought and when the mind wanders you gently bring it back into focus.

Using prayer beads such as rosaries and repeating mantras are examples of concentration meditation techniques, but there are other concentration techniques that you can try.

Monkey mind

In India and Sri Lanka monkeys are often caught using simple traps made out of hollowed out coconuts. The trappers drill two holes into a coconut shell, one small hole just big enough to thread a rope through and knot it, and one just big enough for a monkey to slide its hand inside. They place a treat inside the coconut shell and when the monkey reaches its hand inside and grasps the treat in its fist they reel it in like fishing. The monkey becomes so focused on holding on to the treat inside that it refuses to let go to free itself.

Concentration meditation can be thought of as similar to trapping a monkey. It is giving your total attention to one thing, and not thinking about anything else. With practice we can gradually learn to focus our minds for longer and longer periods of time.

Concentration techniques you can try

Here are some meditation techniques that you can try. See which one works best for you. Start off slowly, set a timer for 5 minutes then gradually over time work your way up to 30 minutes. When you first begin 2 minutes will feel like an eternity, and you will find yourself struggling to maintain your concentration, but gradually it will get easier and easier.

Breath meditation

This is a traditional Buddhist meditation technique.

With your eyes either open or closed, concentrate your attention at the point midway between the eyebrows on your forehead. This is the frontal lobe area of the brain which some people refer to as the "third eye".

Inhale slowly, counting to eight. Hold the breath for eight counts. Now exhale slowly to the same count of eight. Repeat. Be as attentive as possible. Concentrate on the breathing process itself, feeling your diaphragm and chest expanding and contracting. Keep your gaze steady at the point between your eyebrows.

If you find that your mind has wandered, simply bring it back to an awareness of your breath.

Candle flame

The candle flame technique is an open eyed meditation. You simply sit in front of a lighted candle and watch the flame flicker continuously. Relax and blink naturally. Watch the shape of the flame move and change. When your mind begins to wander bring it back to the candle flame. It takes a lot of discipline to simply watch the flame and not make judgments about what you are seeing and begin to see shapes and images in it.

Meditating on a rose

This is both an open eyed and closed eyed meditation. Sit with a rose or other flower in front of you. Concentrate on the shape, the scent, and the colour. Gradually narrow your focus and concentrate on each individual petal, its texture, and the veins in it.

Close your eyes and recreate the flower in your mind. Manipulate the flower mentally, make it larger, make it smaller, feel the texture of the petals, rotate it in your mind. As you get better at this you can mentally change the colour of the flower and practice experiencing the flower with your other senses, for example you could smell the colour. What does the colour red smell like? What does red feel like? Is there a temperature associated with the colour red?

Morphing shapes

This is a closed eye meditation where you project the image of a simple geometric shape like a triangle, a square, or a circle onto the movie screen behind your closed eyes. As you look at the shape it begins to move, to change colour, and then morph into another shape.

The trick with this meditation is to keep yourself simply an observer, letting the shapes change without your participation. Simply observe the changes without consciously manipulating it or making judgments about the changes.

Number concentration

This is my favorite meditation technique. It is very simple and for people who like to measure their progress this method is ideal.

Similar to the morphing shapes meditation this is a closed eye meditation where you project an image onto the movie screen behind your closed eyes. In this case you project the number 1, you examine the number 1 closely and watch it change colour and become more elaborate, then watch it morph into the number 2, then the number 3, and on and on. Keep moving on until you loose concentration and then start back at number 1 and keep going. See how far you can get before your mind wanders and you have to start again.

Dealing with distractions

It is inevitable that you will experience distractions, both external events and internal thoughts that will draw your attention. The ticking of a clock, and the humming of the refrigerator will seem to get louder and louder. Simply tell yourself that these are normal background sounds and gently draw your attention back to the thing you were concentrating on.

It is the difficulty in quieting our minds that is the greatest challenge for most people. No matter how many times your mind wanders simply return to your concentration, be gentle with yourself, don't get frustrated, over time you will find that your mind will wander less and less.

One trick that I have found very useful is to keep a note pad and a pen on a table beside me and when I have a thought that seems urgent and refuses to go away I quickly make a note of it then tell myself that it is not important right now, that I will take care of it at the appropriate time and then return to my concentration.

How long do I need to meditate?

The Dalai Lama spends many hours every day in meditation, but for most of us fifteen minutes or a half an hour daily is about all that we can manage to squeeze into our busy days.

The Sit-Stand Method

If you find that you want to gradually increase the amount of time you spend in meditation you might find the Sit-Stand method useful. In this longer method you break up your meditation time into three fifteen minute sessions that are easier for your body to tolerate. The standing increases your blood circulation which helps keep you awake, and alternating between periods of sitting and standing prevents the muscle cramping and numbness caused by sitting for too long a period of time.

This method is very simple. You meditate in a seated position for fifteen minutes, then meditate in a standing position for two minutes, then sit for another fifteen minutes, stand for two minutes, then sit for a final fifteen minute session. You can time yourself with a timer or by making a tape recording with the sound of a bell to let you known when to stand up and sit down.

Meditation helps you become a better tea leaf reader

Meditation creates a wonderful sense of tranquility and relaxation. Being accomplished at meditating is not required when you first begin reading tea leaves. Anyone can sit down and look for symbols in the tea leaves, but meditation can help you to stay focused and improves your connection to the universal consciousness, resulting in better, more accurate readings.

"If man has no tea in him he is incapable of understanding truth and beauty."

Japanese Proverb

Symbolism 7

Interpreting the symbols

The following are some traditional interpretations of symbols you might find in your tea cup.

These are simply suggestions, don't bother trying to memorize these meanings, just read them over and your subconscious mind will be able to pull them up when you need them. **Also, if the thought that pops into your mind when you see the symbol in a cup differs from these meanings in this book go with your own instinct.**

The universe knows what a particular symbol means to you based on your life experience. For example, I know a woman who is terribly afraid of dogs. She was bitten as a child and is terrified of even the friendliest dog to this day. Obviously if she sees an image of a dog in her tea cup she is going to think of fear even though most people in North America think of dogs as symbolizing a loyal friend, unconditional love, and protection.

I know another woman who dislikes birds, why I have

no idea, but obviously if she saw an image of a bird in her cup she would think dirty and noisy, she certainly wouldn't think good luck, and the ability to soar above your problems. So if any of these interpretations don't feel right to you for whatever reason go ahead and use your own interpretation.

A few keys to interpreting symbols:

Finger - A finger emphasizes whatever sign it points at. In other words, if you see a finger look closely at what it is pointing at, it is saying that this is important.

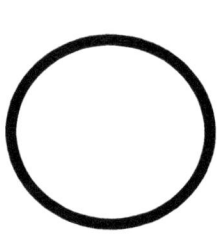

Circle - It is a good omen if another symbol is surrounded by a circle. If the thing it surrounds is a negative symbol it means that the negativity is reduced, for example if you see a cross in a circle (a cross signifying trouble or heartache) it means avoidance of trouble, or that you will be protected from trouble. If the circle surrounds a positive symbol then the good of that symbol is increased, for example if you saw a bunch of dots in a circle that would mean that you are going to get a LOT of money.

Square - A square on its own means restrictions, like you are being boxed in. But if it is surrounding a negative object it means protection from that negative thing. If it surrounds a positive object then it means that something is preventing you from getting the thing you want.

Symbols close to the handle mean that it is close to home, in other words it is something important to the inquirer, something significant in their life at the present time. If it is pointing toward the handle it means that it is coming to the inquirer, pointing away from the handle means that it is something the inquirer is doing to someone else.

Dots always mean money.

Numbers usually refer to timing. For example the number 3 could mean 3 days, 3 weeks, or 3 months depending on the position in the cup. Closer to the top means a shorter period of time. One exception to this would be in the case of someone wanting to know how many children they are going to have. If there was a number beside an image of a basket or of a baby then it probably refers to the number of children.

Letters of the alphabet usually refer to a person's name, but they can also refer to a month.

Timing, if the symbol is at the top of the cup the thing it represents will come quickly. The closer to the bottom the longer it will take.

Drops of tea remaining in the bottom of the cup represent tears.

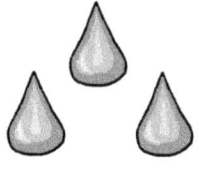

People, when you see people look closely at what they are doing. If they are engaged in an activity, the activity is usually what is significant.

Symbols in alphabetical order

Acorn - An acorn means good news. Financial conditions are improving, or an improvement in health. Something big is going to grow from your present small start.

Airplane - An airplane refers to ambition, a business trip, or a vacation. If the plane is heading toward you, expect an overseas visitor. Obviously if the airplane looks like it has crashed down into the bottom of the cup with the nose of the plane crumpled, it isn't a good sign, but it doesn't necessarily mean a plane crash, it could just be referring to the expression "to crash and burn" as in things aren't going to go as well as you had hoped.

Alligator or crocodile - An alligator represents an untrustworthy friend. Things aren't what they appear. An alligator lying sunning itself can look dead and harmless but don't get too close it can turn on you in an instant.

Altar - An image of an altar symbolizes consolation, or joy. The idea of consolation comes from the Christian idea of turning to Christ (going to the altar) to sooth your pain. In other words, this symbol means that you will get over whatever the problem is. The idea of joy in connection to an altar refers to a joyful ceremony like a marriage.

Ambulance - An ambulance represents injury or illness, but not necessarily serious enough to actually require an ambulance.

Anchor - An anchor is very good luck. It can symbolize rest, relaxation, business success, or resting comfortably after a journey.

Angel - Angels symbolize good news, protection, and happiness.

Ant - Ants represent order, discipline and community activity. Industrious activity, victory through effort, business success gained through your own hard work, but you will experience strong competition.

Apple - Apples represent education, wisdom, knowledge, and great achievements.

Arc - An arc is not a good sign. An arc is basically an unfinished circle. It means that something is unfinished, unforeseen misfortunes, or possible ill health. Look carefully to ensure that it is actually an arc and not a rainbow which is a good omen signifying a happy/sunny future.

Arch - An arch refers to foreign travel, stepping into a brighter future. This is a good omen, but it can also mean that for some time you may have to go it alone.

Ark - A boat like Noah's Ark symbolizes a safe refuge in the midst of trouble.

Arrows - Arrows symbolize unwelcome news, rumors, jealousy, and slander. It could be in the form of a letter or an e-mail.

Axe - An axe symbolizes impending danger, something is going to hit you. Remember, this is symbolic, so it doesn't necessarily mean physical danger.

Baby - Babies symbolize luck in the home, new interests, could mean an actual new baby but not necessarily.

Bag - A bag is pretty obvious, if it appears empty it means poverty, if it appears full it means abundance.

Ball and chain - These prison symbols represent burdensome commitments.

Balloon - Balloons represent a party invitation, an improvement in finances and a release of tension. Like helium balloons floating up high in the sky, this indicates that things are moving up for you.

Ball - A ball symbolizes an opportunity for you to catch, but can also mean ups and downs in finances and relationships depending on the other symbols around it.

Basket - A basket often means that a new baby is on the way, if not a baby then a gift of some kind.

Bat - Bats represent false friends, disappointments, someone will tell you a secret. It can also mean that you are looking at something from the wrong perspective.

Bear - Bears represent a long journey, one in which you will need to depend on your own inner resources.

Beaver - Beavers represent continual hard work. As animals that live in the water, they are associated with dreams and emotions.

Bed - A bed represents comfort, contentment, peace of mind, a new lover or a marriage proposal. If messy and unmade it can refer to mistakes in the past (as in you've made your bed now lie in it), sleepless nights, worry.

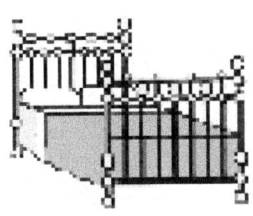

**Bees** - Bees represent enjoyable activity, fertility, productivity, and the sweetness/honey of life. You will be productive and busy, and you may be offered a job. Dead bees mean loss of money.

Bell - A bell is ringing to inform you of unexpected news.

Bicycle - A bicycle can mean travel, but it can also represent achievements reached through your own effort and hard work.

**Birdcage** - If the bird cage is empty and the door is open then you are free to take on new ideas and new projects. If the cage door is closed it represents obstacles and restrictions preventing you from doing what you want to do.

Birds - Birds symbolize good luck especially if they are flying. Good news, you will rise above your problems. Two birds are particularly lucky.

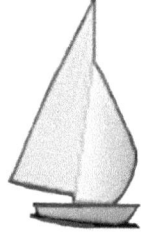**Boat** - A boat can represent overseas travel or a visit from a friend from far away. But it can also represent a new discovery, like explorers discovering a new continent. A sailboat can represent moving fast without effort. If there are big waves around the boat it can indicate stormy seas, or challenging situations.

Bomb - A bomb represents an unpleasant, unexpected event, very sudden.

Boomerang - What you have sown now comes back to you, or as my father used to say "You're getting some of your own back."

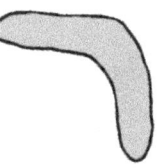

Book - If the book is open it means that important news is on the way, a new chapter in your life now begins. If closed it means that you will have difficulty in getting what you need.

Boot - Getting the boot usually refers to losing your job, but it can also represent deciding to change your partner, or getting dumped by a partner.

Bottle - A bottle often refers to problems related to alcohol, if broken it signifies a quarrel.

Bouquet of flowers - This is a very lucky sign indicating good friends, success, and a happy marriage.

Bow and arrow - Like the arrow alone, the bow and arrow represents unwelcome news, rumors, jealousy and slander being aimed at you. It could come in the form of a letter or an e-mail.

Braid - A braid symbolizes two or more lives intertwined.

Branch - Something new, a branch often refers to the birth of a child, or it can be a new friendship.

Bridge - A bridge represents opportunities, and a solution to a problem. It is a symbol of transition; it means that something you desire to change will change.

Bridle - A horse's bridle means restraint. Either you are being held back, or you should hold yourself back.

Broom - A broom symbolizes sweeping away the old, new conditions are coming in. A negative situation is being brushed aside by the positive actions that you take.

Buckle - A buckle represents frustration, being held back from doing something that you want to do.

Buffalo - The buffalo represents abundance. The hump on its back is symbolic of reserves of energy. A reminder that it is not necessary to push or force, simply to follow the easiest path.

Bugle - Time to wake up, be alert, pay attention to what is going on around you.

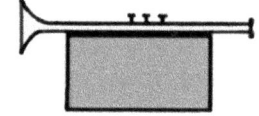

Building - A building or a house can mean a move to a new location.

Bull - A bull represents quarrels among associates, slander and gossip.

Bush - A bush represents a new group of friends, or personal growth.

 **Butterfly** - Butterflies represent transformation, metamorphosis, rejuvenation, lightness and joy. They can also refer to lighthearted flirting and enjoying a period of being a social butterfly.

Cactus - Cactus represents toughness, endurance, stoicism, and courage.

 **Candles** - Candles represent kindness, spirituality, help coming from others, but can also symbolize the flame of passion.

Cane - You will be getting a visit from a discontented, unhappy person.

Cage - Like a birdcage, if the cage door is closed it represents obstacles and restrictions; you are not able to do what you want to do. An empty cage with the door open means that you are free to take on new ideas and new projects, but this could be the result of a marriage breakup.

 **Cake** - Cakes represent celebration, something sweet.

Camel - A responsibility is being placed on your shoulders, it could involve travel.

 **Car** - A car in your cup could mean that your will be buying a new car, or your existing car may need repairs, but it can also refer to travel or visits from friends.

Cart - A cart represents fluctuations of fortune, if full it means abundance, if empty if means hard times financially.

Castles - Castles represent the fulfillment of big goals and expectations. They also represent security, family festivities, and happy events.

 **Cat** - Cat lovers will probably take offense with this, but cats represent sneaky, untrustworthy people, treachery, and hidden agendas.

Cattle - A herd of cattle represent prosperity and contentment. A single cow happily eating grass means a happy home life.

Catapult - A catapult looks like the letter Y with something hanging off it, it usually indicates an unprovoked attack.

Cemetery - Headstones in a cemetery mean death, generally that you will be hearing news of someone's death.

 **Chain** - An unbroken chain can mean marriage and friendship, but if it feels tight it can mean bondage or addiction, if broken it refers to divorce, the end of a friendship, or breaking of a business contract.

Chair - Chairs represent comfort, but also the likelihood of an unexpected visitor or an addition to the family.

 **Cherries** - Cherries usually represent the start of a romance, something very pleasant and sweet.

Chicken - Like the image of a cow, the image of a chicken represents a happy contented home life.

Child - This is an awkward one when you are doing a reading for someone else. Depending on the symbols around it, it could mean a new baby is on the way, or that someone is going to get greater access to a child that they are estranged from, or it could mean that someone is behaving like a child.

Church - Churches represent solemn occasions, like marriages, christenings, or funerals.

Circle - Circles are very good omens, they represent love, success, and completion. If the image is that of a ring it symbolizes marriage.

Claw - Claws represent a hidden enemy, as in "someone has their claws out for you."

Clock - Clocks indicate that timing is important, do not procrastinate. It usually involves important business transactions. You will need to set a date for an important meeting.

Clouds - Dark clouds indicate danger, trouble, confusion, or doubts. It is difficult to see white puffy clouds in a teacup but if you do they indicate release of tension.

Clover - A three leaf clover = good luck in business. A four leaf clover = overall good luck.

Club - A baseball bat or club can represent a weapon which means conflict.

Coat - When you see a coat it means a separation, someone is leaving.

Coffin - A coffin means disturbing news, but does not necessarily mean death.

 **Coin** - This is a good omen, it means that you will be paying off debts.

Column - A tall column or pedestal indicates success while a broken column (like a Roman ruin) indicates failure.

 Comma - A comma indicates a pause of some sort, which can be good or bad depending on the influences around it. It can mean taking time off because you're sick or it can mean relaxing on vacation.

Compass - A compass represents exciting travel to new places, and adventure.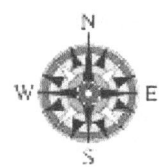

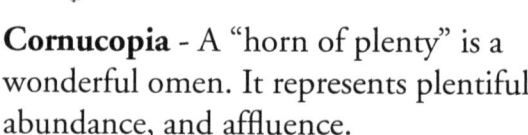 **Corn** - An ear of corn is a symbol of prosperity.

Cornucopia - A "horn of plenty" is a wonderful omen. It represents plentiful abundance, and affluence.

Crab - Can represent a person born under the sign of Cancer.

Cricket - A lucky omen. It means money is coming to you.

Cross - Crosses generally represent emotionally painful situations, heartache, suffering, and sacrifice. As in "this is the cross I have to bear."

Cross in a circle - A cross in a circle means there will be a potentially painful situation but you will be protected from it.

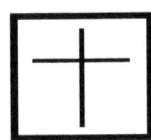
Cross in a square - Having a square around something means that something is being restricted, in this case a cross inside a square means that you will be able to avoid the emotionally painful situation, it means protection from trouble.

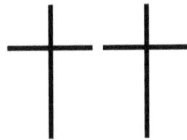
Two crosses - Two crosses are not good, this symbol represents something twice as painful, could represent a severe illness.

Three crosses - Three crosses represents a painful situation that eventually has a favorable outcome.
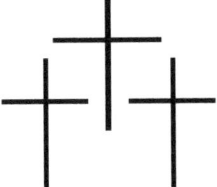

Crown - A crown represents success, spiritual enlightenment, or a promotion at work.

Cup - Cups are very good. They represent abundance, success, happiness.

Curtain - Behind the curtain there is a secret, something you don't currently know or understand.

Daggers - A dagger represents an unexpected enemy, someone you think is a friend will hurt you.

 **Daisy** - A daisy represents modesty, but it can also refer to springtime.

Deer - A deer symbolizes gentleness, innocence, and timidity.

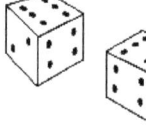 **Dice** - Rolling the dice represents loss, or financial misfortune.

Dog - A favorable sign that means faithful friends and unconditional love. If the dog appears to be barking it is warning you to beware of something.

Donkey - Someone is being stubborn, it could also mean that patience is required on your part.

Door - Doors symbolize a new undertaking, as in you will be opening a new door in your life, but it can also indicate that a door is closed to you.

 **Dots** - Dots clustered together mean money, the more dots the better.

Dove - Doves represent peace of mind and happiness, if two doves together it means a happy marriage.

Dragon - Dragons are fictitious animals, they represent irrational fears, fear of something that doesn't exist, in other words, worrying for nothing.

Drums - Drums represent a loud person, or annoying gossip.

Eagle - Eagles represent people in a position of authority, as in law, government, or politics. They also represent clairvoyance, the ability to see the future, and can represent seeing new opportunities. Eagles have excellent hearing, which can represent clairaudience. Two eagles represent sexual energy, passion.

Ear - An ear can mean that you will hear some surprising news, or that you are being talked about, some malicious rumors.

Easel - An easel represent creativity, creative work.

Eggs - A well formed egg means good luck, but if cracked or broken it means bad luck.

Elephants - An elephant is a symbol of good fortune, especially if the trunk is up. They also represent strength and wisdom, or a reminder not to forget some special day.

Envelope - Envelopes symbolize the coming of long awaited news.

Envelope in a circle - This is extra good news, usually it means that money is coming.

 **Eye** - An eye warns you to look carefully, caution is advised. Something needs to be inspected carefully before you make a decision.

Eyeglasses - Put your glasses on because you are about to get an unpleasant surprise, you are vulnerable to lies and deception, and false friends.

 **Explosion** - A sudden upheaval.

Face - One face represents a new acquaintance, lots of faces mean social meetings or work conferences.

 **Fairy** - Fairies represent romance, adventure, and a joyous life, but they can also mean that you are living a fantasy, believing something that isn't true.

Fan - A fan in a reading always refers to a flirtation. The message is that you should cool it or you will be involved in an embarrassing situation and people will be hurt.

**Feathers** - Although birds represent good luck, good news and rising above your problems, individual feathers are not so good; they represent instability, frivolity, unpredictability and a lack of concentration.

Fences - Fences represent being imprisoned by personal circumstances, but these are temporary difficulties that you can climb over.

**Fire** - Fire represents passion, passionate love, but can also mean a sudden burst of anger.

Fireplace - A fireplace represents contentment, passion under control, a comfortable home, and domestic bliss.

Fish - Fish represent good luck in all things, lots of friends and personal power. If surrounded by dots it means lots of money. It can also represent someone born under the sign of Pisces.

Fist - Anger and impulsive conflict.

Flag - A flag can be a warning of danger, but it can also mean victory.

Flies - Flies or other insects represent minor irritations or minor setbacks.

**Flowers** - Flowers symbolize comfort, joy, personal happiness, good fortune, success, and a happy marriage.

Foot - Important decisions need to be made, you need to make a stand.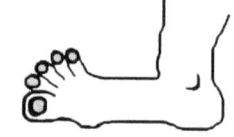

Fork - Getting diverted from your goal, you need to make a choice between 2 or more options.

Fountain - A fountain represents enduring happiness, water (emotion) continually flowing.

 **Fox** - The Fox represents cunning and treachery. They have very keen hearing, vision, and sense of smell. These traits symbolize clairaudience, clairvoyance, and clairgustance.

Frog - Frogs represent a sign of change in health from bad to good or from good to bad. Frogs are also associated with fertility, and success in love.

Fruit - Any type of fruit represents abundance and prosperity.

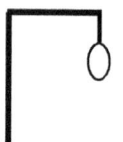 **Gallows** - Gallows are a sign of great danger, don't make sudden or impulsive business or emotional decisions.

Gate - Gates suggest that solutions to your problems will be available. If the gate is open, opportunities will open up suddenly. If the gate is closed opportunities will close suddenly.

Garden - Gardens represent happiness, success, contentment, and a pleasant surprise.

Garlands - Honors will be bestowed on you.

Goat - Nimble and flexible, a goat can also represent a person born under the sign of Capricorn.

Gondola - A gondola represents a romantic liaison, but one that you will soon tire of.

Grasshopper - Grasshoppers represent a lack of foresight, or a visit from a long lost friend.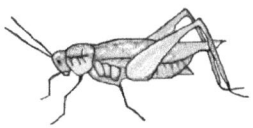

Greyhound - You will be successful as a result of your own strenuous exertion. You will work hard for what you achieve.

Groundhog, or Gopher - Make sure that you always have alternate plans, in other words an exit strategy.

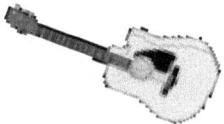
Guitar - Musical instruments are a symbol of harmony, and loving relationships.

Guns - Weapons are a sign of conflict.

Hammer - A hammer is an indication that strong effort will be required, hard work.

Hand - Someone is offering you their hand in friendship, but it can also mean flattery.

Handcuffs - Handcuffs represent problems and constraints.

Hat - You will be putting on a new hat, in other words a new work situation.

 **Heart** - Hearts represent love, romance, marriage, and happy outcomes in emotional issues.

Heron - The heron is a solitary and aloof water bird. Water represents emotions. Therefore, a heron can represent patience and timing particularly in emotional situations.

Hoe - A hoe usually means that you will be rewarded for your hard work.

 **Horse** - Horses represent wealth, romance, and speedy travel. Horse and rider means good news will be arriving quickly regarding financial prospects or romance.

Horseshoe - Horseshoes always represent good luck. If surrounded by dots luck involving money, it may be time to go buy a lottery ticket.

 **Hourglass** - An hourglass indicates that you need to make a decision quickly, do not procrastinate. It can also indicate death, as in "time is up."

House - Houses represent security, future ease and freedom from worry. It can also indicate a move to a new location.

 **Hummingbird** - Hummingbirds symbolize accomplishing what is seemingly impossible, especially with regards to healing long-standing illnesses and problems in relationships.

Insects - Insects represent irritating worries and minor vexations.

Iron - An iron is a good omen, it usually means that things will work out, quarrels will be resolved, problems will be "ironed out".

Ivy - Ivy represents happiness, good friends, and an enduring marriage.

Jug - A jug symbolizes good health, prosperity and a rise in social status.

Jewelry - Jewelry can represent money but it can also represent vanity.

Jockey - A jockey represents good luck, a winning streak, can represent gambling.

Kangaroo - Kangaroos represent a sudden unexpected journey, speed.

Kettle - A kettle symbolizes a happy home.

Keyhole - A keyhole represents unwanted news, something you don't want to see.

Keys - Keys represent new experiences, new doors opening for you, and pleasant surprises.

Kites - Kites represent rising through the ranks to a lofty position, in other words advancement at work. They also represent wishes come true, freedom and being released from problems.

Knife - Knives represent quarrels, or severing a relationship. A knife surrounded by dots means fighting over money.

Ladder - A ladder going up towards the rim represents success, but one going down towards the bottom of the cup represents failure. The number of rungs on the ladder may indicate how many days, weeks, or months before an event takes place.

Lamp or lantern - The light cast from a lamp or lantern indicates a deeper understanding of your karmic lessons, either you have learned your lessons or you are about to.

Leaf - Leaves represent good luck, the more leaves the better, lots of good news.

Letter - When you see a letter it means that you will receive an important document, an initial nearby may indicate the name of the sender.

Lighthouse - A lighthouse represents protection from a storm. You will have some problems, but you will get through them safely.

Lines straight - Straight lines are an indication of peace, happiness, and long life. They also predict a pleasant journey ahead.

Lines wavy - Wavy lines represent troublesome journeys, uncertainty, or losses. The importance of the wavy lines depends upon the number of them and if they are heavy or light. The losses will be greater if they are long, heavy and wavy.

Lion - A lion is a powerful adversary, or a loyal and helpful friend.

Lock - If the lock is open or broken it represents theft, if closed it means there is an impediment or obstacle preventing you from getting or doing something.

Logs - Logs represent heavy burdens but can also indicate stubbornness.

Magnet - A magnet symbolizes being pulled toward something, whether this is good or bad depends on the other symbols around it.

Mailbox or Mailman - An important letter is on the way.

Man - A man standing means that you will have an unexpected visitor. If the man is performing some sort of activity it is the activity that is significant.

Maps - Maps represent a long journey, somewhere that you haven't been before.

Masks - Masks indicate deception, things are not what they seem, someone is hiding something from you.

Masonic symbols - Masonic symbols represent brotherly love, ceremony, honest dealings.

Mermaid - Temptation is beckoning.

Mirror or looking glass - Mirrors represent the development of psychic ability, clairvoyance, and personal growth.

Monkey - Someone is playing with you, they are not sincere. You will be deceived in love.

Monster - There is something you fear, usually the fear is not real, like the monster under the bed when you were a child it disappears when you turn the light on it.

New Moon

Old Moon

Moon - The Moon is a sign of psychic development, in particular clairvoyance. A full moon means a love affair, while a half-moon represents marrying for money. If the Moon illustrated in the cup is new (with its curved side to the right and its pointed ends to the left) a new opportunity will appear before the next new moon. If the Moon is old (with its curved side to the left and the pointed ends to the right) a situation or person will leave you before the next full moon.

Mountain - Mountains indicate struggles or challenges. Big goals mean big challenges.

Mouse - Like a mouse stealing crumbs in a kitchen, this symbol represents theft, loss of money, being cheated.

Mouth - A mouth symbolizes that it is time to speak out.

 **Mushroom** - Mushrooms represent unavoidable delays, then sudden growth.

Needle - A needle suggests that you will be recognized for your achievements, your creativity, and your hard work.

Nest - A nest represents a comfortable, happy home.

 **Net** - A net usually represents a trap, a snare, some sort of hidden difficulties.

Noose - A noose is a sign of danger, something that you will get hung up on.

Numbers - Numbers usually indicate timing, how long before something takes place, but can also represent the number of children.

 **Oak tree or leaf** - Oak is a hard wood and represents a strong constitution and good health.

Octopus - Octopus symbolizes many aspects to a problem, many dangerous complications.

Otter - This water mammal represents joy, playfulness and sharing. They love to play and have a great sense of humor, this can suggest that you need to be more like the otter, or it can represent someone who is happy and playful.

Owl - Some people consider owls to be a very bad omen indicative of sickness, poverty, disgrace, a warning against starting a new enterprise. However, the owl can also symbolize fertility, seduction, magic, darkness, wisdom, prophecy, clairvoyance, and spirit contact.

Oyster or clam - This can represent a person or a situation of a secretive nature, also hidden assets.

Palm tree - Palm trees symbolize good luck, a happy long-term relationship, and success in any undertaking. It can indicate a new baby on the way.

Parachute - A parachute symbolizes a convenient escape.

Parcel - If you see a parcel expect a present. An initial nearby may indicate from whom. It can also represent luxury, and extravagance.

Parrot - Parrots represent people talking, gossip. Can also be a sign that you will be relocating for a lengthy period.

Peacock - Peacocks represent found money, success and the acquisition of property. It can also indicate vanity and a love of luxury.

Pear - All fruits symbolize abundance. Pears in particular represent great wealth, success in business, and improved social position. It can also represent marrying for money.

Pentagon - A pentagon (five-sided) symbolizes intelligence and education.

People - When you see people, look carefully at what they are doing, and interpret their actions literally. Look for initials and numbers close by to tell you who the people are and when the events will happen.

Phoenix - A phoenix rising from the ashes symbolizes making the best of a bad situation, something you thought was lost is coming back, it turns out that something wasn't a failure after all.

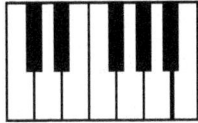

Piano - All musical instruments represent harmony and the piano in particular represent different people working together to achieve a common goal.

Pig - Pigs represent intelligence, prosperity, and possible greed.

Pillar - A pillar is like a column, if tall and well formed it indicates being given recognition of an achievement, if broken like a ruin it represents a failure that will negatively affect your reputation.

Pine cone - Pine cones are symbols of fertility.

Pipe - A pipe symbolizes problem solving through creative ideas. Think Sherlock Holmes.

Plow - A plow represents a new project that you will undertake shortly.

Priest - A priest symbolizes spiritual leadership, and helping others in trouble.

Pumpkin - Pumpkins symbolize growth and change, also autumn.

Purse - Obviously if the purse is empty it represents poverty or lose of money, but if full it indicates plenty.

Pyramid - A pyramid represents a desire for immortality, and the common fear of death.

Question mark - Question marks represent confusion and difficulty making a decision.

Rabbit - Rabbits symbolize timidity, phobias, and fears. This symbol indicates that there is a need for bravery

Rainbow - The rainbow is a very lucky symbol which represents protection, the end of troubles and a secure future. The difference between an arc and a rainbow is that the arc has only one ring, it isn't finished.

Rat - Rats represent success, shrewdness, abundance and adaptability. But rats can also mean cheating, treachery, and loss.

**Ring** - A ring symbolizes engagement and marriage, if a letter is found near it, this could be the initial of the future spouse. A broken ring symbolizes divorce. If clouds are near the ring, it symbolizes an unhappy marriage.

Roller coaster - These represent the ups and downs of life, fluctuations in fortune, or emotions.

Rope - There are restrictions hampering your activities, if the rope is tangled you will experience complications.

Rose - All flowers are good luck, in particular, the rose represents love and artistic success.

Ruins - Not a good sign, ruins usually indicate a reversal of fortune, a business failure.

Saddle - "Get back in the saddle", means get back to work. You will be working hard at something ambitious.

**Saw** - A saw in your tea cup represents upcoming trouble or a dispute with a stranger.

Scales - Scales always indicate dealings with the law. There will be a favorable outcome if the scales are balanced.

Scarecrow - A scarecrow represents irrational fears.

Scepter - A scepter represents increasing responsibilities at work.

 **Scissors** - Scissors indicate quarrels, loss of a friend, and separation from loved ones.

Scorpion - A scorpion represents a dangerous rival, a plot, jealousy, and lies.

 **Shark** - A shark represents a threat, danger.

Sheep - Sheep are a good omen representing success, and prosperity.

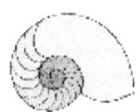 **Shell** - Shells mean good news is on the way.

Ship - Ships represent good luck in business affairs, and a successful journey.

 **Shoe** - Putting your best foot forward, polishing up your shoes, time for a change in career.

Shovel - Shovels indicate that you are preparing the groundwork for something big, lots of hard work and physical exertion.

 **Skeleton** - Skeletons refer to a period of ill health or financial hardship.

Skull - A skull represents danger in your path.

Skunk - Because of its smell, the skunk does not have to get out of the way of any animal; it is self assured, confident, and silent. The skunk symbolizes respect and self-esteem.

Sleigh - A sleigh symbolizes rapid and easy advancement, if on a hill it means that it will be VERY fast.

 **Snail** - Things will not be moving as quickly as you would like, also the snail represents someone with a slow and plodding nature.

Snake - Snakes represent transformation, healing, wisdom, and the awakening of creative forces. When provoked snakes strike fast, beware of spiteful enemies.

 **Spider** - The spider represents creativity, perseverance, building and rebuilding. It can also mean that money is coming soon.

Spiral - A spiral represents a slow but certain rise. If it looks more like a tornado the rise will be much more rapid, sweeping away everything in its path.

 **Spoon** - A spoon represents generosity, and sharing.

Staff - A shepherd's staff indicates that you will be taking on more responsibility.

Stairs - Like a ladder, stairs going up toward the rim represent success, but one going down towards the bottom of the cup represents failure. The number of steps on the stairs may indicate how many days, weeks, or months before something takes place.

Star - A star is a very lucky sign; if it is surrounded by dots it means great wealth and recognition.

Shooting star or comet - Means that what you wish for will come true.

Submarine - Submarines represent secret enemies, treachery, something that you don't know about that is hidden under the surface.

Sun - The sun is a very good sign, it represents long-term happiness. However it can also mean taking a sunshine holiday, something good will happen in the summer, or it can represent someone born under the sign of Leo.

Sword - Swords represent disputes, quarrels with close friends, and lovers' quarrels.

Table - Tables represent a pleasant social gathering.

Teapot - Teapots represent social gatherings and important business meetings. It is telling you to speak your mind openly and fearlessly.

Tent - Tents represent unforeseen adventure, travel, and an opportunity to get away for a while.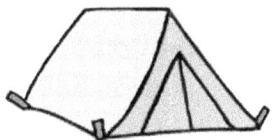

Tower - A tall well formed tower represents security, but a cracked or leaning tower indicates disappointment, the security you thought you had is about to collapse.

Thistle - The emblem of Scotland, it represents a tough person who can survive anything, anywhere.

Throne - Thrones represent a change of position, advancement, or a promotion in the workplace.

Tornado - Tornados represent rapid upward movement that sweeps away everything in its path.

Trees - Trees are a lucky sign; they represent prosperity, growth, expansion, realization of goals, and recovery from illness.

Triangle - A triangle is always a sign of good luck, unexpected events, and unexpected legacies (inheritances).

Tunnel - A tunnel symbolizes coming through a dark period in your life, but now you are coming out into the light. Your future is about to get brighter.

Turtle - Turtles represent criticism, pulling into your shell, sticking your neck out, things will be slow in coming.

Umbrella - You will have numerous small worries, but will be sheltered from any real adverse conditions.

Unicorn - A unicorn is a mythical creature, it represents believing in a beautiful fantasy.

Volcano - A volcano symbolizes a sudden loss of control, passion.

Vulture - Vultures represent patience, waiting for your opportunity, and then taking advantage of it.

Wallet - If the wallet is full then money is coming, if empty then money will be lost.

Watch - Like the clock, watches indicate that timing is important, do not procrastinate. It usually involves important business transactions. You will need to set a date for an important meeting.

Waterfall - A waterfall represents the flow of abundance, you will be receiving a steady flow of money, could be a very secure job, or a pension.

Web - A web symbolizes a complicated dilemma, deceit, something that can trap you or confuse you, getting caught up in something that isn't good.

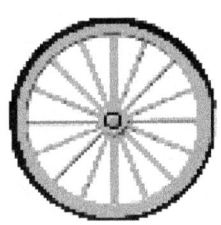**Wheel** - A wheel generally represents progress, good results, and good fortune. However, it can also symbolize the wheel of fortune or wheel of chance where you never know what fate has in store for you, uncertainty.

Wheelbarrow - A wheelbarrow represents self-reliance. You can do it yourself.

**Wildcats** - Wildcats are solitary nighttime hunters, known for their stealth, silence, and good eyesight. They are able to see what others try to hide. They represent danger, secrecy and intrigue.

Windmill - Windmills represent success in business through your own hard work.

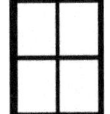**Window** - Looking through the window your future is looking brighter and happier.

Wine glass - Wine glasses represent new friends, celebrations, and over indulgence.

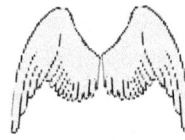**Wings** - Wings indicate that a message is on its way, also that the situation will change quickly.

Wolf - A wolf warns you to beware of jealousy and fraud.

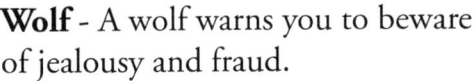

Worms - Worms indicate secrets, intrigue, and hidden situations.

Yoke - A yoke represents slavery, addiction, domination, need for strong will

Zebra - Zebras represent adventures in foreign lands.

Playing card symbols

Clubs - Clubs are like Pentacles (coins) in the tarot deck. They represent money, or business affairs, new enterprises which will be a success.

Diamonds - Diamonds are like Wands in the tarot deck. They represent travel, creativity

Hearts - Hearts are like Cups in the tarot deck. They represent affairs of the heart, and emotions.

Spades - Spades are like Swords in the tarot deck. They represent disagreements, illness, or actions that need to be taken. You need to make a decision.

Zodiac Symbols

When you see a Zodiac symbol it could be referring to aspects of the inquirer's personality, the personality of another person who figures prominently in the issue at hand, or the month that an event will take place.

 **Aries** - The Ram, March 20 to April 19, energetic, impulsive

 **Taurus** - The Bull, April 19 to May 20, determined, stubborn

 **Gemini** - The Twins, May 20 to June 21, sociable, intellectual, two sided

 **Cancer** - The Crab, June 21 to July 22, caring, emotional, perfectionist

 **Leo** - The Lion, July 22 to August 23, flamboyant, extravagant, generous

 **Virgo** - The Virgin, August 23 to September 22, helpful, analytical

 **Libra** - The Scales, September 22 to October 23, sensitive, loves beauty and harmony

 **Scorpio** - The Scorpion, October 23 to November 22, passionate and intense

 Sagittarius - The Archer, November 22 to December 21, optimistic, impulsive, generous

 **Capricorn** - The Goat, December 21 to January 20, successful, stable, patient

 **Aquarius** - The Water Pourer, January 20 to February 18, independent, intelligent, and confident

 **Pisces** - The Fish, February 18 to March 20, emotional and mystical

8

Sample Readings

The readings on the following pages are examples of readings done for family members and friends using different types of tea.

Reading #1

This reading was done with a type of green tea that has large pieces of leaf and stems so the images were large.

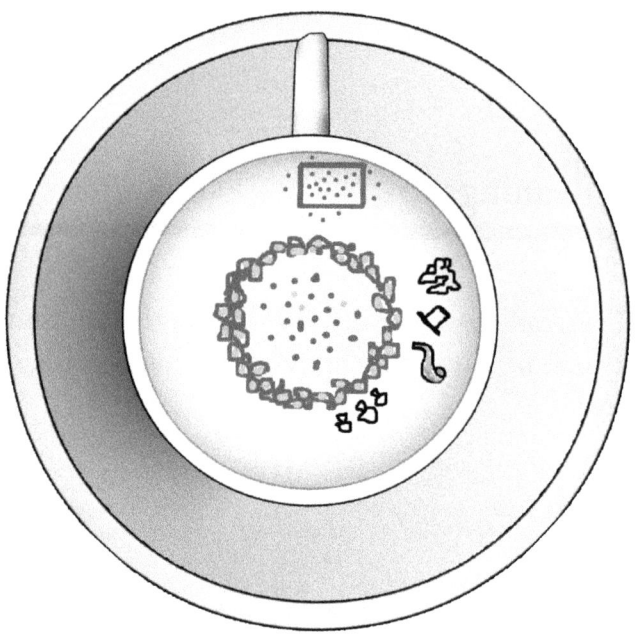

Symbols

As soon as I looked at the cup it was immediately apparent that this person had money and job concerns because near the rim, close to the handle was a box with dots inside it. An image that appears in the top portion of the cup, near to the rim indicates that this is something that is happening at the present time. That it was close to the handle indicated that it was something that is very close to the person, or something that the person was very concerned about.

Dots are usually a very good sign, a sign of money,

but in this case there was a box surrounding the dots. This indicates that the money was being hampered, in other words you couldn't get at the money. There were a few dots outside the square, but most were inside it.

On the bottom of the cup however was a very clear image of a garland of flowers. This is a good omen indicating honors being bestowed. In this case it was particularly good because it seemed to be forming a circle around another group of dots. I was surprised to see this many dots in a reading with this type of green tea since it isn't chopped up as finely as many other teas.

About midway down the side of the cup there was what looked to me like a map, which indicates taking a trip. Near the map there was what appeared to be a top hat and a pipe. Below that, toward the bottom, there appeared to be 3 mushrooms.

Interpretation

I interpreted this to mean that the querent was very concerned about money and employment, which is a very common concern. Because the dots were inside a square it was apparent that the money was there, but the person couldn't seem to access it. The querent acknowledged that she was very frustrated with the bad year she was having in her consulting business. Many contracts that she had submitted proposals for had not panned out, and the clients she did have were paying very slowly. The small number of dots outside the square represented the small amount of revenue that was presently coming in.

The map part way down the side of the cup suggested that she would be taking a trip somewhere she hadn't been before. The hat nearby suggested that it would be a business trip, that it was a top hat suggested some sort of performance. In this case because of the nature of the querent's business I interpreted this to mean that she would be going to a different city to perform for an audience (in this case convince prospective customers to hire her). The pipe suggested that she needed to come up with some creative solutions to her customer's problems.

The 3 mushrooms suggested that there would be a period of time of unavoidable delays where nothing would appear to be happening and then there would be sudden growth. I interpreted this to mean that she should keep on putting out feelers, in other words sending out promotional materials and talking to prospective customers and that within a short period of time (possibly 3 months time) her business would take off.

The garland at the bottom of the cup represented recognition and respect. I interpreted this to mean that she would eventually become highly respected in her field and the money that she deserved would come as a result of this.

There were no tea leaves in the saucer so that was the end of the reading.

Reading #2

This reading was done using Rooiboos, or red tea. This is not really tea, it is a caffeine free herb from South Africa that many people enjoy as a tea substitute. It is primarily small twigs ground very fine and so the images can be difficult to see. I knew this person, but not particularly well, (a friend of a friend) so I was not familiar with the recent events in her life.

Symbols

As soon as I looked into this cup the first thing I noticed is that there were a few drops of tea left in the bottom of the cup. This is usually interpreted as tears. In this case I immediately got the sense that these tears had already been shed, in other words the pain that had caused the tears was something recent, not necessarily something in the future. I asked the querent if she had recently been emotionally upset and crying and she acknowledged this.

The next thing I noticed was what appeared to be a basket up near the rim of the cup, but it was enclosed in a box. A basket often symbolizes a baby on the way, but the box suggested that something was preventing this from happening.

A little farther around the cup there appeared to be a brick wall, a coat, and a woman and man embracing behind a curtain.

On the other side of the cup I noticed what appeared to be 2 doves and some flowers.

Finally down on the bottom of the cup there was a baby carriage, the number 2, and the letter J.

There was a trail of grounds (I would normally have called these tea leaves, but in this case because it was Rooiboos it was more like very fine sticks or needles) where the residue had been poured into the saucer. This looked like a funnel or a marker pointing up.

I noticed that there was an image in the saucer as well, but the saucer would be read only after I finished reading the cup itself.

Interpretation

The basket in the box and the tear drops in the cup suggested that the querent had been wanting a baby but something was preventing it from happening.

The brick wall and the coat indicated that there was a stubborn situation and someone was leaving. The querent acknowledged that she and her fiancé had recently broken up because they could not come to an agreement regarding having children. She felt that her biological clock was ticking away and that she was running out of time to have children but he claimed he wasn't ready.

The curtain suggested that there was something else about the situation that was hidden from her. The image of the man and woman embracing behind the curtain suggested to me that there was another woman involved, that the fiancé's real reluctance to get married and have children had something to do with his involvement with another woman.

The image of the 2 doves and the flowers on the other side of the cup indicated that eventually the querent would find a new love and be happily married. She currently wasn't involved with anyone new and was too devasted by the recent breakup to imagine who it could be so it is possible that she doesn't know this person yet. That it was around on the other side of the cup indicated that it was around the corner, something she couldn't see from her present vantage point, but that it was coming soon enough.

The image of the baby carriage, the letter J, and the number 2, on the bottom of the cup I interpreted as meaning that she would have a baby in 2 years, however it could also have meant that she would eventually have 2 children. The letter J would be significant in her life at that time.

The Saucer

Now it was time to see what the saucer had to tell us. There was a blob of grounds in the center of the saucer with splashes of grounds radiating out of it. This looked to me like the rays of the sun. I interpreted this as meaning that after this painful period she was presently going through the sun would come out and she would once again be happy.

Reading #3

This reading was done with a variety of green tea that was made up of relatively large leaves.

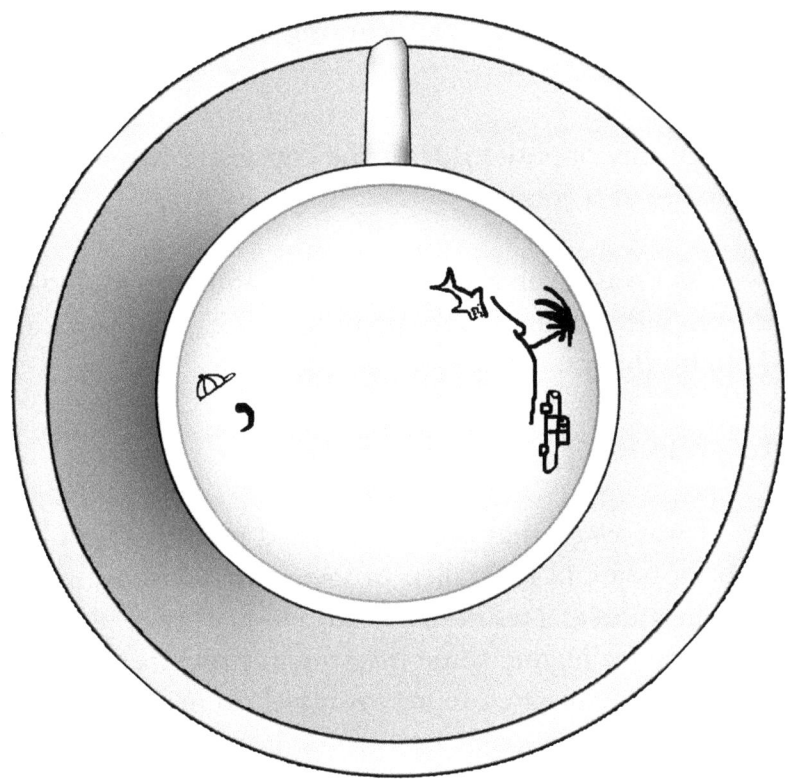

Symbols

The first thing that I noticed when I looked into this cup was that very few of the tea leaves had stayed in the cup after it had been turned over into the saucer making this a very fast cup to read.

What was clearly visible was a very distinct picture of a palm tree and a tropical beach. A seemingly beautiful idyllic looking setting located about midway down the side of the cup. But then I realized that the setting wasn't quite as idyllic as it had first appeared because I noticed a shark just below the surface of the water.

Then I noticed a car pointing toward the palm tree and the tropical beach.

On the opposite side of the cup was a hat, and what appeared to be a comma.

As I was turning the cup around and around, looking at it from different angles, the palm tree fell over and appeared to fall into the water.

Interpretation

I was aware that the querent had recently taken a car trip to Florida and had fallen in love with the sunshine and the beaches and as a result of the drop in real estate prices was thinking about buying some investment property there. The image of a car can often represent travel, so in this case I felt that the car and the palm tree on the beach represented this trip and the plan to purchase Florida real estate.

Usually palm trees represent good luck and success in an undertaking, but in this case the fact that the palm tree fell over made it seem to me that this real estate purchase might not be such a good idea.

The shark reinforced this opinion. Sharks represent danger. In this case it seems that there is danger lying beneath the surface of this seemingly idyllic setting.

Hats represent a change in work duties. I was aware that the querent's career was in a creative field that often involves periods of unemployment between contracts. In this case I interpreted this hat to mean that the querent would be changing jobs, and this job change might mean that his income might not be as steady.

A comma represents a pause, things might not happen as quickly as you hope.

I suggested to the querent that perhaps he should investigate very carefully before making any real estate decisions at this time.

The Saucer

The majority of the tea leaves had fallen into the saucer when the cup was turned over resulting in what looked like a pile of hay with a pitch fork in it. I interpreted this to mean that the new work situation would be in a different field and would involve a lot of hard work but would ultimately be financially profitable.

Reading #4

This reading was done using loose English Breakfast tea, which is a blended tea chopped into pieces. It is an excellent tea to do readings with because the pieces are larger than those in tea bags and yet smaller than many green or white teas resulting in easier to read images.

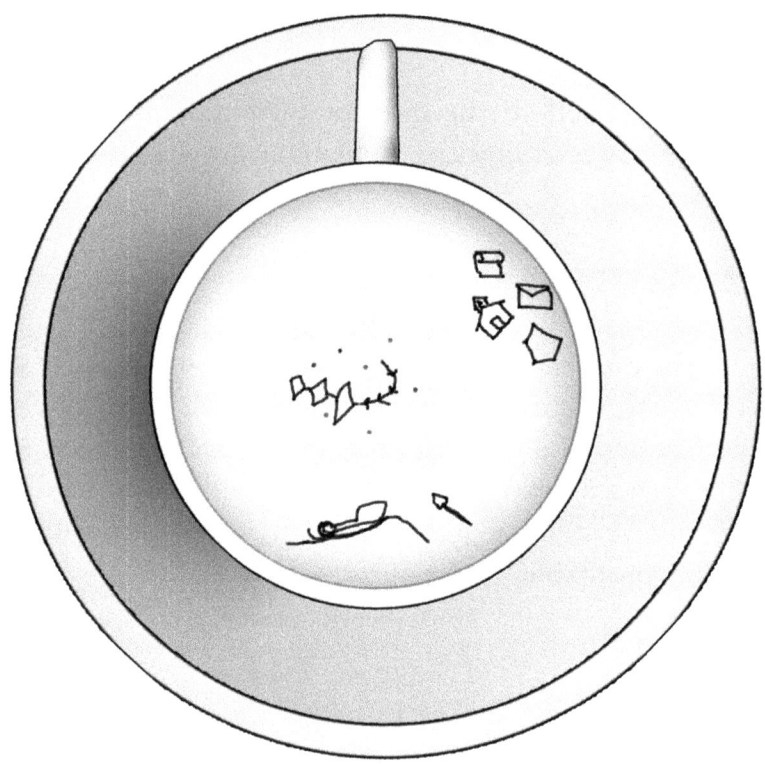

Symbols

The first symbols that I noticed when I looked into this cup were a school house accompanied by an envelope, a certificate or letter, and a pentagon (5 sided figure) about half way down the side of the cup.

A little further around the cup I saw a shovel, and a sleigh or toboggan on a hill. At the bottom of the cup was a kite that appeared to be flying in the breeze. The kite was surrounded by dots.

Interpretation

A school house, an envelope, a certificate and a pentagon, obviously this person has education in their future.

A school house always refers to education, either the person is going to be attending school or they are a teacher. In this case I knew that the querent was not a teacher so perhaps she would be taking some courses in the near future. This was backed up by the pentagon, which is a five sided figure that refers to intelligence and education, and the certificate or diploma. An envelope means that good news would be arriving soon. I interpreted this to mean that the querent would soon be going back to school.

A shovel usually means working hard and preparing the ground for something new. In this case I interpreted that to mean that for the querent going back to school would mean working hard, but that this would prepare her for something great in the future.

The sleigh or toboggan on a hill means rapid advancement, or moving fast.

Finally, the kite flying in the breeze represents advancement at work and your wishes coming true. Dots always mean money.

No tea leaves had fallen into the saucer which meant that was all there was to the reading.

So for this querent I felt very confident in predicting that she would be returning to school, she would be earning a diploma, and that this would be very good for her career and her finances in the future.

Reading #5

This reading was done using a regular tea bag which I cut open with a pair of scissors and poured loosely into the cup. After much experimentation I have found that when using tea bags it is best not to use the entire tea bag in one cup because it is just too much fine powdery tea floating around to enjoy actually drinking the tea. However, using less tea does result in a weaker cup of tea.

Although many people use tea bags exclusively, and do excellent readings with them, I find that the images are a bit muddier than when you use a good quality loose tea.

Symbols

The following symbols were randomly situated around the sides of this cup:

- A noose
- A net
- A web
- A broken bottle
- A broken heart
- Several question marks

At the bottom of the cup was a large Y, or a fork in the road.

Interpretation

A noose, a net, a web, and a broken heart are not nice, happy symbols. A noose refers to danger. A net is a trap or a snare, it also symbolizes danger. A web symbolizes deceit, confusion, and getting caught up in something that isn't good.

A broken bottle usually refers to quarrels and problems related to alcohol.

The question marks symbolize being unsure of yourself and having difficulty making decisions.

The broken heart is pretty much self-explanatory. Someone is hurting emotionally.

The large Y on the bottom of the cup could be someone's initial or it could mean a fork in the road. I asked the querent if the letter Y was significant to her in any way. Did she know anyone with this initial? She couldn't think of anyone or anything significant so, considering the other symbols in the cup, I concluded that it meant that she was at a cross road in her life, that it was time for her to make some decisions.

I pointed out the question marks in her cup and asked her if she was having difficulty making a decision about something. She explained that she had been dating a married man who had been claiming that he was in the process of leaving his wife, but that now she wasn't sure that she believed him. I pointed out the broken heart and suggested that lots of hearts would be broken if she continued with the relationship.

The broken bottle is a tricky symbol to discuss with someone. Since it refers to alcohol problems it can be a difficult to know exactly how to approach it. In this case because I knew the querent quite well I simply asked if there was anyone in the situation that seemed to have a drinking problem. She acknowledged that she was starting to suspect that the man she was dating had a drinking problem.

I pointed out that there were no symbols of a happy relationship or marriage in her cup so maybe she should take a good look at what she had gotten herself involved in and make some difficult decisions.

The saucer

Some of the tea fell into the saucer when the cup was overturned. It formed what looked like a dark tunnel. I explained that although she was going through a particularly difficult time at present, if she made the right decisions she would come out the other end of the tunnel into a brighter future.

Appendix A - Money Symbols

Good	Bad
+ A **full bag** means money is coming	**-** An **empty bag** means lack
+ A **full wallet** means money is coming	**-** An **empty wallet** means poverty
+ A **full purse** means prosperity	**-** An **empty purse** represents lack
+ A **buffalo** represents abundance	**-** Dead **bees** lying on the bottom of a cup mean a loss of money.
+ A **coin** represents paying off debts	**-** **Dice** represent financial loss
+ **Cattle** represent prosperity	

Good　　　　　　　　Bad

+ **Corn** represents prosperity

+ A **cornucopia** represents prosperity

+ **Crickets** mean that money is coming to you

+ **Dots** always mean money

+ Any kind of **fruit** represents prosperity and abundance

+ A **jug** represents prosperity

+ **Peacocks** represent money and luxury

+ A **spider** can mean that money is on its way

+ A **waterfall** can mean that a steady flow of money is on its way

− A **knife surrounded by dots** means fighting over money

− An **owl** can represent money problems

Appendix B - Love Symbols

Good

+ A **ring** represents engagement or marriage

+ **Hearts** obviously represent love and romance

+ An **altar** can represent a wedding

+ A **bed** can represent a new lover, or a marriage proposal

+ **Flowers** represent joy and a happy marriage

Bad

− A **broken ring** symbolizes divorce

− A **broken chain** can represent divorce

− A **boot** can represent getting dumped by a lover

− A **sword** represents a lover's quarrel

− A **knife** can represent the severing of a relationship

− A **coat** represents separation, someone is leaving

Good

+ A **braid** can represent a marriage, two lives intertwined

+ **Cherries** represent the start of a romance

+ A **church** can symbolize a marriage

+ An **iron** means that problems in a relationship will be ironed out

+ A **rose** symbolizes love

+ **Two doves** together symbolize marriage

+ A **palm tree** can represent a happy long-term relationship

Bad

− A **monkey** means that someone is playing with you romantically, they are not sincere

− **Pears** can mean marrying for money

− A **gondola** represents a romantic liaison, fun, but it won't last

Appendix C - Children Symbols

+ Obviously, **a baby or a child** can mean that someone will be having a baby, but not necessarily

+ A **basket** can mean that a baby is on the way

+ A **branch** often means that a new baby is on the way

+ A **palm tree** can mean that a new baby is on the way

+ **Pine cones** are symbols of fertility

Appendix D - Health Symbols

Never make predictions regarding another person's health. These symbols are intended only for looking into your cup for information regarding your own health.

+ Acorns can mean that health is improving

+ Trees represent recovery from illness

+ A **jug** represents good health

− Ambulances represent illness or injury

− An **owl** can represent sickness

− A **skeleton** represents a period of ill health, not death

+ − A **frog** represents a change in health, either from bad to good, or good to bad

Appendix E - Honesty Symbols

Good

+ A **lion** represents a powerful adversary or a faithful friend.

+ **Masonic symbols** represent honesty.

Bad

- **Alligators or crocodiles** indicate untrustworthy people

- **Arrows** represent gossip and slander

- **Cats** represent sneaky, untrustworthy individuals

- A **curtain** represents a secret that is being kept from you

- A **claw** represents a hidden enemy

- **Daggers** mean that someone you think is a friend will hurt you

- A **fox** represents cunning and treachery

- **Masks** indicate deception, something is hidden

- A **monkey** represents an insincere person

- An **oyster or a clam** indicates that something is hidden

- **Scorpions** represent lies and dangerous rivals

- **Snakes** can represent spiteful enemies

- **Submarines** represent secrets hidden under the surface

- A **web** indicates deceit

- A **wolf** is a warning of jealousy and fraud

- **Worms** indicate secrets, intrigue, and hidden situations

- **Eyeglasses** mean that you need to look carefully, you are vulnerable to lies deception and false friends

"Drink your tea slowly and reverently, as if it is the axis on which the earth revolves - slowly, evenly, without rushing toward the future."

Thich Nat Hahn

Index

A

abstract pattern recognition 2-4, 8-9
accuracy 9-10
acorns 80, 140
airplane 80
alcohol problems 133
alligator 80, 141
alphabet 79
altar 81, 137
ambulance 81, 140
American Revolution 29
anchor 81
angel 81
ant 81
antioxidants 27
antique cups 17-18
apple 81
Aquarius 116
arc 81
arch 82
Aries 115
ark 82
arrow 82, 141
artists 11
audio recordings 52-53
axe 82

B

baby 82
baby carriage 122-124
bag 135
ball 83
ball and chain 82
balloon 82
basket 83, 122-124
bat 83
bear 83
beaver 83
bed 83, 137
bees 84, 135
bell 84
bicycle 84
birdcage 84, 87
birds 77-78, 84
black tea 31
blended teas 35-36
boat 84
bomb 84
book 85
boomerang 85
boot 85, 137
Boston Tea Party 29
bottle 85
bouquet 85
bow and arrow 85
box 118, 122-124
braid 85, 138
branch 85
breath meditation 71
brick wall 122-124
bridge 86
bridle 86
Britain 10, 28-29, 49
broken bottle 132-134
broken heart 132-134
broom 86

bubbles 41
buckle 86
Buddha 27
Buddhist monks 28
buffalo 86, 135
bugle 86
building 86
bull 86
bush 86
business cards 57-58
business decision making 11
butterfly 87

C

cactus 87
caffeine 35
cage 87
cake 87
camel 87
Camellia Sinensis 30-37
Cancer 91, 115
candle flame meditation 72
candles 87
cane 87
Capricorn 116
car 87, 126-127
cart 88
castle 88
catapult 88
cats 88, 141
cattle 88, 135
cemetery 88
censoring your comments 23

certificate 128-130
chain 88, 137
chair 88
cherries 88, 138
chicken 89
chicken bones 14
child 89
children 24, 139
China 27-28, 30
Chinese legends 27-28
chlorophyll 34
Christians 19
church 89, 138
circle 78, 89
clairvoyance 102
clam 104, 142
claw 89, 141
clock 89, 112
clouds 89
clover 89
club 90
clubs 114
coat 90, 137
coffee ground divination 2
coffee shops 48
coffin 90
coin 90, 135
column 90
comet 110
comma 90, 126-127
compass 90
competition 58
concentration meditation 70-75
consumer protection legislation 49
corn 90, 136
cornucopia 90, 136
cows 88

crab 91
creativity 11, 15
credit cards 54
crickets 91, 136
crisis and drama 20-22
crocodiles 80, 141
cross 91
crown 91
cup 92
curtain 92, 122-124, 141

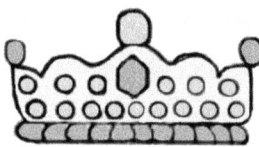

D

daggers 92, 142
daisy 92
Dalai Lama 74
D-Day 50
death 7, 23
deer 92
demonic possession 21
diamonds 114
dice 14, 92, 135
divination 1
divorce 107
dogs 77, 92
donkey 92
door 92
dots 79, 92, 118-120, 136
doves 93, 122-124, 138
dragons 93
drama and crisis 20-22
drops of tea 80, 121
drums 93
Duncan, Helen 49-51

E

eagle 93
ear 93
Earl Grey tea 35-36
easel 93
Edinburgh Scotland 50
Edwards, John 6, 14
egg 93
elephant 93
emotional problems 21
English Breakfast tea 35-36, 128
envelope 128-130
explosion 94
eye 94
eyeglasses 94, 142

F

face 94
fairy 94
fan 94
feathers 95
feet 96
fences 95
fermentation 31-36
finger 78
fire 95
fireplace 95
fish 95
fist 95
flag 95
flame divination 1
flavoured teas 36
flies 95
flirtation 94
flowers 85, 95, 122-124, 137

foot 96
fork 96, 132-134
fountain 96
fox 96, 142
frog 96
fruit 96, 136

G

gallows 96
garden 96
garland 96, 119-120
gate 96
Gemini 115
Ginger root tea 37
Gissing, George 12
glasses 94, 142
goat 97
God 19, 59
gondola 97, 138
gopher 97
grasshopper 97
green tea 31, 33, 118, 125
greyhound 97
groundhog 97
guitar 97
guns 97

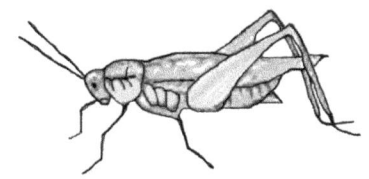

H

hammer 97
hand 97
handcuffs 97
hat 97, 126-127
health department regulations 48
health questions 23-24, 140
hearts 98, 114, 137
herbal infusions 37
heron 98
HMS Barham 50
hoe 98
Holland 28
home parties 60
honesty 24, 141
horn of plenty 90, 136
horse 98
horseshoe 98
hot wax divination 1
hourglass 98
house 98
hummingbird 98
hunches 11

I

imaginary friends 15
imagination 2-5
Infinite Spirit 19
insects 98
insurance 48
intention 19-20
intuition 2-5, 13
iron 99, 138
ivy 99

J

Japan 28, 30
jewelry 99
jockey 99
jug 99, 136, 140

K

kangaroo 99
Kava root tea 37
kettle 99
keyhole 99
keys 99
kite 99, 129-130
knife 100, 136-137
Kukicka 34

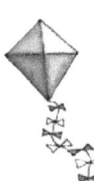

L

ladder 100
lamp 100
lantern 100
Lapsang Souchong tea 36
leaf 100, 103
Leo 115
letter 79, 100, 128-130
Lewis, C.S. 26
Libra 115
Licorice tea 37
lighthouse 100
lines 100
lion 101, 141

lock 101
log 101
looking glass 102
love symbols 24, 137-138

M

magnet 101
mailbox 101
mailman 101
man 101
map 101, 119-120
masala tea 36
mask 101, 142
Masonic symbols 101, 141
mediums 6-7, 13
mediumship 6-7, 13
meditation 67-75
mermaid 101
metaphysical bookstores 48
mindfulness meditation 70
minister 49
mirror 102
mirror gazing 10-14
money 24, 135-136
monkey 102, 138, 142
monkey tea 28
monster 102
moon 102
morphing shapes 73
mountain 102
mouse 102
mouth 102
mushrooms 103, 120

N

Native American teachings 20
needle 103
needy clients 54
nest 103
net 103, 132-134
noose 103, 132-134
number concentration 73
numbers 79, 103

O

oak leaf 103
octopus 103
oolong tea 31, 34
orange pekoe 32
ordained minister 49
otter 103
outdoor fairs 64
owl 104, 136, 140
oxidation 31-36
oyster 104, 142

P

palm reading 47
palm tree 104, 125-127, 138
parachute 104
parcel 104
parrot 104
peacock 104, 136
pears 105, 138
pentagon 105, 128-130
people 80, 105
phoenix 105
physical medium 51
piano 105
pig 105
pillar 105
pine cone 105
pipe 105, 120
Pisces 116
pitchfork 127
plane 80
plow 106
Portsmouth England 50
post-fermented tea 33
pouching tea 34
prayer 18
prayer beads 70
priest 106
privacy 21, 53-54
psychic fairs 61
psychics 6-7, 13, 15, 47, 49
psychological problems 21
psychometry 18
pu-erh tea 33
pumpkin 106
purse 106, 135
pyramid 106

Q

question marks 106, 132-134

R

rabbit 106
rainbow 106
rat 106
reading body language 4
red tea 31, 35, 121
Reiki 70
ring 107, 137
ritual 16
roller coaster 107
Romans 1
Rooiboos tea 35, 121
rope 107
Rorschach test 9
rose 107, 138
rose meditation 72
ruins 107
Rune stones 14
Russian Caravan tea 35-36

S

saddle 107
Sagittarius 116
sailboat 84
saw 107
scales 107
scarcity 58
scarecrow 107
scepter 107
schizophrenia 6
school house 128-130
scissors 108
Scorpio 116
scorpion 108, 142

Scottish medium 49
scrying 10-14
self destructive behavior 11
shark 108, 126-127
sheep 108
shell 108
ship 108
shoe 108
shooting star 110
shovel 108, 129-130
silk tea bags 40
silvertip pekoe tea 34
sit-stand meditation 75
skeleton 108, 140
skeptics 56
skull 108
skunk 109
sleigh 109, 129-130
snail 109
snake 109, 142
South Africa 35
spades 114
spider 109, 136
spiral 109
Spirit guides 5-6, 16-17, 19
Spiritualism 7, 15, 19
Spirituality of Money, the 66
spoon 109
square 78
Sri Lanka 30, 71
staff 109
stairs 110
star 110
street festivals 64
subconscious mind 9, 16, 77
submarine 110, 142
sun 110, 124
superconscious mind 8-9, 13, 20, 43
sword 110, 137
symbolism 77-116

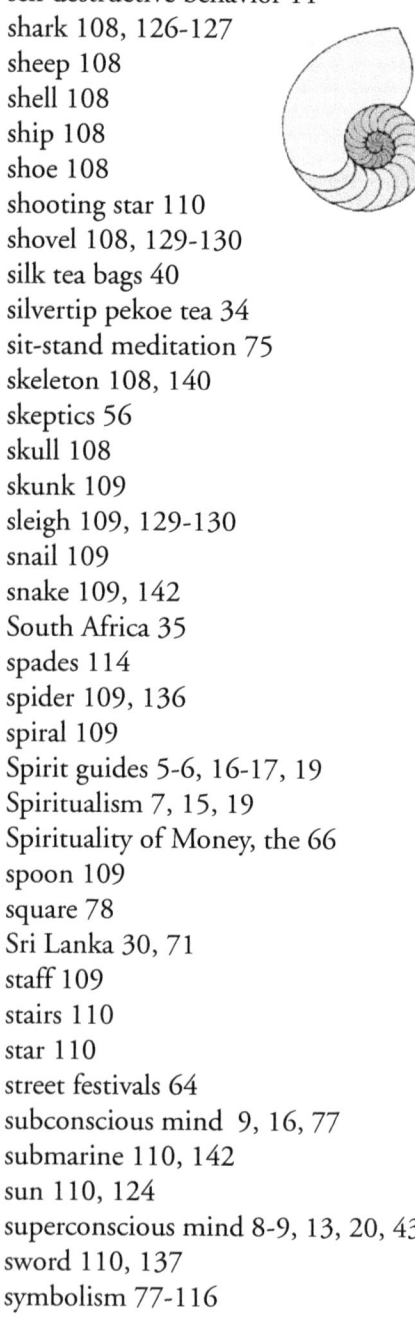

T

table 110
Tarot cards 6, 10, 14, 47
Tasseography 1
Taurus 115
tax deductions 59, 65
tax evasion 65
tea bag 131
tear drops 80, 121
teapot 110
tent 111
third eye 72
thistle 111
throne 111
timing 79
tisanes 37
tower 111
trees 111, 140
triangle 111
Trickster Spirits 20
tunnel 111, 134
turtle 111

U

umbrella 112
unicorn 112
United States of America 49
Universal Consciousness 5, 8-9, 13, 20, 43
Universal Energy 19
Universal Intelligence 59
Universal Mind 5, 8-9, 13, 20, 43

V

Virgo 115
volcano 112
vulture 112

W

wallet 112, 135
watch 112
waterfall 112, 136
web 112, 132-134, 142
wheel 113
wheelbarrow 113
white needle tea 34
white tea 34
Wicca 19
wildcats 113
wilting 30-31
windmill 113
window 113
wine divination 1
wineglass 113
wings 113
winter tea 34
Witchcraft Act of 1735, the 49
wolf 113, 142
Woods, Tiger 13-14
working from home 59
worms 114, 142

X - Y	Z
yoke 114	zebra 114 zodiac signs 115

Also by the author:
The Sweat Lodge is For Everyone

ISBN 978-0-9737470-6-5 $19.95

The Native American Sweat Lodge Ceremony offers so many benefits, both spiritual and physical for anyone who has the opportunity to take part in one.

This book is the non-Native's guide to understanding, participating in, and benefiting from Native American Sweat Lodge ceremonies.

To learn more about the author visit:
www.irenemcgarvie.com

To discover more books about personal development, spirituality and divination visit:

www.learnancientwisdom.com

www.ingramcontent.com/pod-product-compliance
Ingram Content Group UK Ltd.
Pitfield, Milton Keynes, MK11 3LW, UK
UKHW021311180426
11947UKWH00015B/1156